How to Start, Operate and Market a Freelance Notary Signing Agent Business
Revised 3rd Edition

by Victoria Ring
Certified Notary Signing Agent
and Certified Paralegal

Second revised printing: September 2004
Third revised printing: February 2005

ISBN 0-9761591-0-4
(previously published by Gom Bizpress, ISBN 1-932966-03-X)
Library of Congress Control Number: **2004112264**
(previously published by Gom Bizpress, LCCN 2004106019)

ATTENTION CORPORATIONS, UNIVERSITIES, COLLEGES, AND PROFESSIONAL ORGANIZATIONS. Quantity discounts are available on bulk purchases of this book for educational, gift purposes or as premiums for increasing magazine subscriptions or renewals. Special books or book excerpts can also be produced to fit specific needs.
For information, please contact Graphico Publishing, 1601 West Fifth Avenue, Suite 123, Columbus, Ohio 43212-2303. Phone: 614.801-9977 or www.graphicopublishing.com.

Graphico Publishing
a subsidiary of 50 State Notary
1601 West Fifth Avenue, Suite 123
Columbus, Ohio 43212-2303

Email: victoria@graphicopublishing.com
Internet: http://www.graphicopublishing.com

Dedication

This book is dedicated to the honor of my savior, the Lord Jesus Christ. He has provided me with many blessings including personal experiences and life-lessons I lived through that enabled me to write the information in this book that will now benefit you.

Books are words that preserve the thoughts and experiences of the author. So although I will leave this life one day, my thoughts and experiences in this book will continue to live on. By honoring Jesus Christ in my work, I can continue to witness to others even after I have gone to live in my heavenly mansion.

From the profits of sales by 50 State Notary, 10% is donated as tithing each month to one or more of the following ministries which I believe to be truly led by the Holy Spirit:

Dr. Peter S. Ruckman
Bible Believers Church
PO Box 6102
Pensacola FL 32503-6102
http://www.kjv1611.org/

Dr. Gail Riplinger
AV Publications, Corp.
PO Box 280
Ararat, VA 24053-0280
http://www.avpublications.com/

Dr. Kent Holvind
Creation Science Evangelism
29 Cummings Road
Pensacola, FL 32503
http://www.drdino.com

**There are only two ways
to change a person's mind:**

1. If they agree with you.
2. If you use forceful fear tactics.

My desire is that you will understand the reasoning and logic behind various ways to build your notary signing agent business. It is my personal hope that you will agree with me after you have absorbed all the information I present in this book. If a writer must use force and intimidation to get his or her point across, there is no growth and the reader will gain nothing from the experience.

Victoria Ring
Author

How to Start, Operate and Market a Freelance Notary Signing Agent Business
Revised 3rd Edition

by Victoria Ring
Certified Notary Signing Agent
and Certified Paralegal

50 State Notary

http://www.50statenotary.com

For all the hard working and dedicated notaries throughout the United States who wants to build a successful freelance business working as a notary signing agent for mortgage, title and signing companies.

Section 1 - Getting Started and Doing Your Job

Table of Contents - Page 2

Table of Contents - Page 3

Section 3 - Marketing Your Business

Table of Contents - Page 4

Section 4 - Other Ways for NSAs to Make Money

Table of Contents - Page 6

Section 5 - Questions and Answers from NSAs

Section 6 - Web Site References

Introduction

When you hear the words "notary public" do you normally think of someone who notarizes car titles in the neighborhood for $1 or $2? If so, it probably never crossed your mind that a notary public could start a successful business for less than $100 and earn $2,000 to $8,000 or even more per month working out of their home.

However, thousands of notaries across the United States are doing just that every single day. Some of them still notarize car titles for $1 or $2, but many of them work as notary signing agents and earn from $50 to $125 for every assignment they complete for mortgage, title and signing agent companies. Plus, there are thousands of mortgage, title and signing companies eager to hire notaries as soon as they receive their notary commission.

This book is truly one of a kind. It will provide you with everything you need to know in order to be successful in a notary signing agent business of your own. The material in this book is written by Victoria Ring, a Certified Notary Public who began her own notary signing business in 2001 when the notary signing agent job nitch first developed. Therefore, you are getting first-hand information from someone who learned this business from the "school of hard knocks." Presently, Victoria is still operating her online notary business which can be viewed at http://www.50statenotary.com; further providing you with evidence a notary signing agent business can grow and become successful. The author says: *"If I can do it — you can too!"*

This book is divided into six sections that are designed to help you start and succeed in the notary signing agent business:

Section 1 – Getting Started and Doing Your Job

This section covers all the beginning and basic information about the notary signing agent business. It will provide answers to questions such as what a notary signing is, how to become a notary and a complete overview of the mortgage documents as it relates to the notary signing agent. (The NNA also offers an excellent review of the mortgage documents in their Certification training course).

Section 2 — Setting Up Your NSA Business

This section begins by exposing the three biggest myths about starting your notary signing agent business as well as a wide variety of tips and techniques for properly setting up your home office. Excellent information about securing a domain name as well as the need for a web page to use in your internet marketing are also provided.

Section 3 — Marketing Your Business

Even if you are the best notary signing agent on the planet, you will not make money unless you learn how to market your business. This section covers a variety of marketing techniques specifically with the notary signing agent in mind. You start by developing a mindset for marketing, then move on to understanding the basics of marketing and end with learning basic internet marketing techniques.

Section 4 — Other Ways for NSAs to Make Money

This section reveals several excellent ideas for expanding and boosting your income as a notary signing agent. Some of these ideas include a step-by-step guide for conducting a title search online or at your local courthouse and how to turn this knowledge into a separate business. Also included is how to start a signing company where you employ other notaries to work for you, as well as how to directly work for mortgage and title companies – thereby eliminating the signing company (middle person) entirely. A variety of additional ideas are also provided so you can expand your services and make additional money.

Section 5 – Questions and Answers from NSAs

This section provides you with a wide range of actual questions, covering a variety of subjects, from notaries across the United States. The answers provided will help you to build and grow your business and help save you from MAKING some of the same mistakes others have made.

Section 6 - Web Site References

This book would not be complete without a healthy supply of additional web site references so that you can take the knowledge you learn from this book and advance your career.

Okay let's get started. I am sure you are as anxious to find out about the notary signing agent business as the author is to share her knowledge with you.

"Let all bitterness, and wrath, and anger, and clamour, and evil speaking, be put away from you, with all malice: And be ye kind one to another, tenderhearted, forgiving one another, even as God for Christ's sake hath forgiven you."

Ephesians, Chapter 4, Verse 31-32

SECTION 1

Getting Started and Doing Your Job

"Lay not up for yourselves treasures upon earth, where moth and rust doth corrupt, and where thieves break through and steal: But lay up for yourselves treasures in heaven, where neither moth nor rust doth corrupt, and where thieves do not break through nor steal: For where your treasure is, there will your heart be also."

Matthew, Chapter 6, Verse 19 thru 21

What is a Notary Signing Agent?

A Notary Signing Agent (hereinafter referred to as **"NSA"**) is a notary public that notarizes mortgage documents for borrower(s) who are either purchasing new real estate or refinancing their current mortgage. A NSA works as an independent sole-proprietor directly for mortgage, title and signing companies. Due to the increase in homeowners' refinancing their homes, and other people purchasing homes because of the low interest rates, a giant competitive market has developed between mortgage lenders and title companies to offer the "best deal" to borrower(s). With this boom in business for lenders, coupled with the changes to the Uniform Commercial Code ("UCC") laws, the NSA job nitch was first developed in early-2001.

Perhaps you can remember the loan process prior to 2001. Back then, if you purchased or refinanced a piece of real estate, you had to travel to an office (at a time the lender set for you), sign your documents, obtain two witness signatures and have the documents notarized. But in 2001, the new UCC law removed the "two witness signature" requirement on mortgage documents. This enabled a notary public to be able to travel to a borrower(s) home and notarize the loan documents without the need for two additional witnesses. Not only did this save lenders a great deal of time and money, it also was more convenient for the borrower(s). Because borrower(s) could now enjoy the convenience of having their mortgage documents signed at their home, mortgage companies offer this service as standard practice when enticing borrower(s) to apply for a mortgage loan.

Now that you know what a NSA is, let's find out how to become a notary public and review the NSA's role in the mortgage loan process. This way you can determine if you would enjoy opening up a business of your own providing NSA services to borrower(s) in your area.

How Do You Become a Notary Public?

The only prerequisite to working as an independent NSA is that you must be a notary public unless you live in the state of Georgia. In the state of Georgia, you must be an attorney to be an NSA, but non-attorneys may still be notaries in the state of Georgia. In all of the remaining 49 states, all that is normally required for you to become a notary public is that you need to be 18 years of age and a resident of the state. How do you become a notary public? It's easy. Go to http://www.nationalnotary.org/, then select "Become a Notary" from the menu list. Next, select your state, read the requirements for becoming a notary public in your particular state and obtain the contact information for a notary application to begin the process. Every state varies in their procedures to become a notary public so be sure and read the specifics about your state and follow their guidelines.

After you have become a notary public and have passed the state specific test (similar process as studying and passing a driver's test), you will receive your notary commission certificate. (Note: Some states do not require you to take a test and other states only have you fill out an application and take it to a Judge for his or her signature). But regardless of your state's procedure, once you have met the requirements, take the certificate to your local court for filing. The clerk will administer an oath of office, file and date stamp your certificate and you are now a notary public and permitted to order your notary stamp.

A notary stamp can be obtained from any office supply store like Staples or Office Max, or you can order them through a wide variety of sources. Go to any search engine on the internet and type in the search words "notary supplies" to start shopping. Notary supplies include items such as business cards, notary journals, thumbprint imprinters, bonds, seals, etc.

Join the National Notary Association

As soon as you have taken your oath of office and your notary certificate has been file-stamped by the court, I highly recommend that you join the National Notary Association ("NNA"). I do not receive a commission from this recommendation, so my opinion stated here is completely unbiased.

One reason I strongly suggest you join the NNA, is because if you are going to become a NSA, you can also take a test to become "certified" and get listed at SigningAgent.Com, located on the internet at http:// www.signingagent.com. Getting listed in this directory will bring you a constant stream of work from the mortgage, title and signing companies. The cost to join the NNA is very low, so I urge you to go online to http://www.nationalnotary.org/, select "Membership" from the menu list and become a member.

After joining the NNA, you will receive your membership number. Then go to http://www.signingagent.com/,
click on "Become a Member" and sign up. You will be
asked for your NNA membership number, so be sure to
have this handy to enter into the membership form.
After signing up with SigningAgent.Com, and getting
listed in the national database, you are now exposed to
a large market of mortgage lenders and title companies
who hire freelance NSAs to notarize loan documents.

How to Get Work Without Joining the NNA

Joining the NNA is by far not the only way of getting
assignments from mortgage, title and signing companies. There are hundreds of directories on the internet
filled with links to companies seeking NSA's. Normally,
the mortgage, title or signing company has a form on
their website that the notary fills out and faxes back to
them along with a copy of their notary certificate. One
such directory is available on my website that I keep
updated on a daily basis. The directory is free to access
and it is located at http://www.50statenotary.com/
directory/company_listing.html.

Contacting mortgage, title and signing companies
yourself will help you to start earning money as soon as
you become commissioned as a notary and receive your
notary stamp. And remember, you earn from $50 to
$125 per signing for about two hours of work.

If you do decide to use directories to sign up online
with mortgage, title and signing agent companies, here
are a few tips that will help you:

Tip Number 1

Before signing up with any company for notary work, you first need to find out if they are seeking notaries in your area. If the company only covers Orange County California and you are located in Huron County Michigan you will be wasting your time signing up with them and will never receive a call. So before signing up with a company you need to do either of the following:

▶ If the company has a website, visit their website and look it over. Click on all the links and look for an "about the company" section so you can find out what areas the company covers and to familiarize you with their operations. If you do not agree with any of their payment or processing policies (such as they only pay a maximum of $20 or something), don't waste your time signing up with them. Find companies you want to work with.

▶ If the company can only be contacted by email, send them a inquiry message like: *"I am interested in signing up with your company as a notary signing agent. I am located in the Franklin county area of Ohio. Please let me know if you serve clients in this area and if so, what are your procedures for signing up with your company? Thank you for your time and consideration. (Your name, address and telephone number)."*

▶ If the company can only be contacted by telephone, call them during normal business hours and ask them what areas they cover. Some companies prefer to be contacted by phone because they can find out your level of professionalism by speaking with you directly. Therefore, make sure the kids are not demanding your attention, the dog is not barking and the television is turned off when you make your call. Conduct yourself in a professional manner and make a good first impression. If you have no skills in professional business behavior, go to the internet and find the hundreds of free articles on this subject and study them. One place to start in order to obtain tips for nonverbal behavior is at http://www.selfgrowth.com/articles/Albright2.html but there are lots more.

Tip Number 2

Once you have determined the company you wish to sign up with covers your area, you need to follow their specific instructions for signing up with them for notary jobs. Some companies prefer you fill out a form on their website, others will email you the forms to print, fill out and fax back to them, and others will use a combination of both. During this phase you also need to find out the following:

▶ What is the average pay range for each assignment you complete?

▶ How often does the company issue payments to notaries? (Bi-weekly, monthly, quarterly, etc.)

▶ Do you receive partial payment if the mortgage signing is canceled?

▶ Will documents be delivered by email or mailed to you by overnight mail?

▶ Will the company supply the copy of all the mortgage documents for the borrower(s) or will you be responsible for making copies? If you will be responsible for the copies, find out how much extra you are paid for this additional service. (Do not allow the company to take advantage of you by not paying you for the copy fees).

The company normally supplies most of this information as a "fact-sheet" when you sign up to work for them. If this information is not provided, you need to call them and get the answers. When you call, remember to be professional and don't take an attitude that the company works for you. Do not make demands and become nasty. Some notaries do this and then wonder why the company never calls them for work.

Be humble in your business dealings. These companies are your customers and should be treated like you would treat the "big" boss for any company you have worked for. Learn how to control your personal feelings. If you become irritated or angry with a company, hang up the phone, take a "time out" and try again.

Remember the old saying: *"Never let them see you sweat."* Compose yourself and conduct yourself like a professional business person who cares about the quality of their work and this silent message will be conveyed through your voice to the company, resulting in more work for you.

Tip Number 3

Once you have completed the company sign-up process — which normally includes filling out an application form and W9 tax form; supplying copies of your notary certificate, driver's license and proof that you have Errors and Omissions insurance — place all the documents, as well as the fact sheet (if provided by the company) into a standard file folder and label it with the company's name. Each company you sign up with should have a separate folder in your office files. This allows you easy access to company contact information and helps you to keep organized and increase your efficiency.

If you sign up with a company and you do not hear from them within 30 days, you can quickly locate the contact name and fax number in your file. Fax, call or email the contact person at the company and let them know you are still available for work. You might want to say something like:

> *I signed up with your company on July 5, 2004 and have not heard from you since that time. Perhaps there have not been any signing assignments in my area, which often happens. However, I would appreciate you considering me for the next signing assignment in the following counties of: (List the counties you serve).*

Often, a simple contact like this one will move your name up on the list of notary contacts that the company keeps. Or, you might try faxing a copy of your resume along with a cover letter stating you are anxious to work for them and a short paragraph as to "why" they should choose your services. These steps also show that you are serious about your work and therefore you will probably be more conscientious of the quality of your work.

Tip Number 4

Be persistent and be prepared to spend some time (hours and days) signing up with the mortgage, title and signing companies so you can start earning money as quickly as possible. Many people will visit a few websites, fill out a few forms, then sit back and wait for their phone to ring. But building a business working as an NSA doesn't work this way. When I first started my business, I signed up with about 200 companies so I could build a steady stream of future work. After signing up with every company directory I could locate, I then went to a search engine and typed in search words like: "notary sign up form," "notaries needed," "notary public jobs" "seeking notaries" and even "notary signing agent jobs." I spent hours going through these links and finding excellent places to sign up for potential assignments. This technique was well worth it. All it cost me was my time and three years later, I am still getting 4 or 5 calls every week from companies that found me from the postings I did back them.

Now that you know how to get work as a NSA, let's learn more about the job itself.

How Does the Mortgage Loan Process Work?

The first thing that happens in the mortgage loan process is the borrower(s) decide to obtain a loan or refinance their current real estate. Today, most borrower(s) go online and search for the best mortgage rates they can find and locate lenders that offer them the best deals. Others will call their local bank or credit union they do business with to start the process. But regardless of the method chosen, once the borrower(s) have decided to purchase or refinance their real estate, and have located the best interest rate and lender they want to work with, they will complete a loan application.

Once the loan application is approved several things begin to happen. Normally the mortgage company is the one that begins the preparation of the documents and arranging for the title search. In some areas, an attorney will perform this function so don't be alarmed if the sequence of events I am describing here changes slightly from mortgage company to mortgage company. I am giving you a general overview of what "normally" happens in the average mortgage loan process so you can understand your role as a NSA and how you fit in.

Next, an appraisal is done. The mortgage company normally does this appraisal but some smaller mortgage companies hire this job out to independent contractors. Appraisals typically cost several hundred dollars and this fee is included on the HUD Settlement Statement the borrower(s) sign when NSAs do a mortgage signing.

After the appraisal (or during the same time period) a title search will be ordered. Some larger mortgage companies will do their own in-house title search, or they may hire this job out to an independent contractor.

Now the mortgage company prepares the mortgage documents, which can contain anywhere from 25 to 150 pages. When all the proper documents have been prepared and the appraisal and title search are completed, the final step is to have the documents signed by the borrower(s). Some mortgage companies (and even title companies) have their own independent notaries who work exclusively for them. Other mortgage and title companies hire a signing company to dispatch the notary to handle the final process.

If a signing company gets the assignment from the mortgage or title company, they will look for a notary in the state where the borrower(s) are located to carry out the execution of the documents so the loan can be closed. This is where YOU (as an NSA) come into the picture. Without you – the documents cannot be properly executed and the loan will not close. Therefore, your role is very important in the loan process – but you are still at the "bottom" of the list in the whole scheme of things.

Because notaries are at the "bottom" we sometimes suffer problems such as signing companies going out of business and not paying us, documents not arriving on time and cancelled appointments we are not aware of. All of these things can cause a NSA to become very frustrated and take their anger out on the entire industry. Hopefully, this book will help you to understand how to prevent problems like this from happening and improve your income in the process.

Why is it Important to Know Where the NSA Fits in The Mortgage Loan Signing Process?

It is vitally important for you to understand how you, as an NSA, fits into the mortgage loan process in order to do your job correctly. Not only does this knowledge give you the "edge" in dealing with the various mortgage, title and signing companies – but it opens doors for you to advance your notary career by exposing you to areas of the real estate field you may be interested in pursing.

Also, knowing where your role as a NSA fits into the loan process will help answer many of the questions that arise when you do your job. For instance, when the signing company does not get the documents to you on time – do you immediately blame the signing company? If you didn't know that the signing company receives their paperwork from the mortgage or title company, it would appear the signing company is the one responsible – when this is probably not the case.

I received an email from a gentleman one day who was very angry and upset that the signing company he had accepted an appointment for had changed the signing date on him. He had accepted the appointment for Wednesday at 2:30 pm but the signing company called and said the appointment had been moved to Thursday at 3:30 pm. This notary got very upset at the signing company and accused them of not caring enough about him to schedule the appointment at a time convenient for him. Needless to say, this notary lost all future work with the signing company.

Why? First of all, it was probably not the fault of the signing company that the appointment was changed. If this gentleman would have understood "where" the notary fit into the big picture, he may have understood the dilemma the signing company was in and handled the situation differently. There could have been any number of reasons this appointment was changed from Wednesday to Thursday. Some of these reasons could have been:

▶ The borrower(s) may have had an emergency come up and changed their closing date.

▶ The mortgage company may have found an error on the HUD Settlement Statement that needed corrected at the last minute.

▶ The mortgage company may have forgotten an important document that needed to be made part of the loan package before the closing and without it the loan would not close.

▶ The title company may not have completed their title search on the day the closing was scheduled – or they may have discovered a lien had been previously overlooked and needed paid before the loan closed.

Of course this is a very short list of the possible reasons why this particular loan date was changed. But keep in mind that most of the time, these problems are NOT the fault of the specific person who called you to go to the appointment. Often, this person is in the same boat you are in. They can only do their job when the mortgage and title companies do theirs. It would be worthless to send a notary out (and pay them) if the documents were not correct only to have the corrected documents resigned again and another appointment scheduled. Instead, the company will wait until the documents are as accurate as possible so they only have to send out the notary one time.

Accepting Your First Assignment

The mortgage lender, title or signing company will call you when they have a loan closing in your area. They will provide you with the location, date and time of the signing. If you are available to do the signing at that date and time, you can make the decision to accept the assignment. However, make absolutely positive that you can follow through. If there is the slightest doubt you cannot meet this appointment, you need to pass this signing by and ask to be considered for the next one.

QUICK TIP

You will not lose future work if you turn down an assignment. Instead, network with another notary in your area and use each other as "backups". Give their name and phone number to the company when you are not available.

If you accept an assignment and cannot complete it for whatever reason, the mortgage company could lose the transaction and the borrower(s) may have to start the entire process over again. As a notary, YOU are very important to the loan signing process, so make sure you take your job seriously.

If you decide to accept the assignment, you should then discuss your fee. Some companies will pay as low as $50 and others pay as much as $125 (or more if you have to drive a greater distance to the borrower(s) home). This fee is negotiable. For instance, I had a company call me to do a signing that required a round trip of 75 miles. When they offered me $50, I explained the extensive travel that would be required and they raised my rate to $90. I accepted their offer and completed the signing.

Finally, after you have agreed upon your fee, you should ask the company if they are going to overnight the mortgage documents to you or deliver by email. If the documents are sent by email, you are normally paid $20 to $30 extra because you must print out two copies of the documents that are emailed to you in PDF or other type of format. You also are responsible for mailing the documents back to the lender by overnight mail. The company will provide you with their UPS or Fed-X account number so you don't have to pay the shipping costs but you should keep a supply of UPS and Fed-X envelopes and labels on hand. They are free for the asking at http://www.ups.com and http://www.fedex.com.

If the company states they will mail the documents to you by overnight mail, your job is much easier because everything (including the pre-addressed envelope to mail back the documents) should be included in the

package. You should receive this package ideally the
day before the signing — but I have experienced many
times when I didn't receive the documents until the
morning or afternoon of the signing date.

Contacting the Borrower(s)

Once you accept the assignment, the mortgage or
title company will normally fax you a confirmation. The
confirmation will provide you with the name, address
and telephone number of the borrower(s). Pay close
attention to the date and time of the appointment and
mark your personal calendar accordingly so you don't
forget.

A day or two before the appointment (if possible),
you need to personally contact the borrower(s). Introduce yourself as the notary and obtain driving directions
to the borrower(s) home. Also confirm the appointment
time with the borrower(s). If the borrower(s) wish to
change their appointment time, you can change the
time but NOT the date of the signing. Keep in mind that
the signing MUST be completed the day the documents
are dated for. Although there is nothing wrong with
changing a signing appointment from 11:00 am to 2:00
pm, it is not permissible to change a time from 8:00 am
Wednesday to 8:00 am Thursday.

Before hanging up the phone, be sure to provide the
borrower(s) with your telephone number. This way, the
borrower(s) can contact you if an emergency arises or
they decide not to go through with the signing appointment. This little tip will save you a great deal of prob-

lems, lost time and lost money if an appointment needs to be canceled. Never travel to a signing appointment until you have spoken with the borrower(s). (I even call them a second time when I am getting ready to leave my office to make sure no problems have came up).

QUICK TIP

You also may want to tell the borrower(s) what color and type of car you will be driving. Explain to them that you are doing this to protect them from any unauthorized persons entering their home pretending to be a notary. Although it may sound extreme, with the inability of cordless phones to be totally private, some weirdo could overhear your appointment arrangements and show up prior to your arrival, gain entrance to the person's home and victimize them. Just by providing the color and type of car you have could actually save a person's life. Think about it.

What To Do When the Documents Are Received

For your first signing assignment, you should allow yourself enough time to go through the documents carefully before you meet with the borrower(s). You may want to use "Sign Here" stickers to indicate every

area where the borrower(s) need to sign and place a
yellow sticky note on the pages that need to be notarized. Be sure NOT to get the documents out of order.
Many lenders arrange their documents in a specific
order, so use a binder clip to secure the pages if necessary.

One of the main documents that arrives separately
(many times it is faxed to you at the last minute) is the
HUD Settlement Statement. HUD stands for **H**ousing
and **U**rban **D**evelopment. This document may either be
two or three pages in length and it and outlines all the
costs involved in the loan. Become familiar with this
document. You might even want to read it over once to
understand the information included on it. Some lenders
may even ask you to fax them back a copy after you
have returned from the appointment to verify the signing has been completed.

The important lines to check on the Settlement
Statement BEFORE you meet with the borrower(s) are
Lines 303, 1601 or 1604 (depending on which type of
Settlement Statement you have). In some cases, the
borrower(s) will need to supply a cashier's, certified
check or money order (made out to the mortgage
company) at the time of the notarization. By checking
Lines 303, 1601 or 1604 of the Settlement Statement
first, you will know if these funds need to be collected.
This way you can inform the borrower(s) and allow
them enough time to go to their bank to obtain the
certified funds. You will return the cashier's, certified
check or money order to the mortgage company when
you send back the documents so the loan can close.

Your First Appointment With Borrower(s)

In most cases you will be traveling to the borrower(s) home to complete the signing of the loan documents. In some cases you will be asked by the mortgage company to drive to their office and the borrower(s) will meet you there. Still, in other cases, I have had a representative from the mortgage company meet me at the borrower(s) home. Personally, I love when this happens. This way, the borrower(s) can ask the representative any questions about the documents since, as a notary, we are unable to provide any legal-related information. It also aides in helping the appointment go much smoother.

What do I mean by "smoother?" *"Do you mean to tell me there are some signing appointments that are not red wine and roses?"* Yes! Because you are limited as a notary to answer any legal-related questions about the loan documents, except to point out where information can be found; many borrower(s) will take longer to go through each document and read them thoroughly. Some borrower(s) will compare numbers on the loan documents with figures they were previously quoted by the lender, which is understandable. Even a small mistake like one-quarter of a percent can make a big difference to borrower(s) who are financing a home. Depending on the amount of the loan, the difference of one-quarter of a percent could actually result in a loss of many thousands of dollars. Although you cannot blame the borrower(s) for taking time to review the mortgage documents (since there is a lot of money at stake here), you don't want a one-hour appointment to turn into a five-hour appointment.

If the borrower(s) do have questions, you are to direct them to call the lender. The lender should have previously provided you with their toll-free number to use during and after business hours. This way, the borrower(s) can call them during the signing appointment, get their answer and proceed with signing the documents.

Another method to use, so the borrower(s) do not have to make several phone calls to the lender, is to assure them they have a right to cancel for any reason within three days of signing. This span of time is called a "rescission period." It begins the next day (other than Sunday) after the documents are signed. Let the borrower(s) know that you will be leaving a copy with them of the documents they signed. They are encouraged to review them, flag any documents they have questions about, then call the lender and get all their answers at one time after you have left. If the borrower(s) are not satisfied after contacting the lender, they can cancel the loan at that time.

QUICK TIP

A 3-day rescission period is only provided for a refinance. A non-owner, unoccupied property does not have a 3-day rescission period.

Document Signing Procedures

When you enter the borrower(s) home it is polite to comment on what a nice home they have or make small talk about the weather. Be extremely courteous, cheer-ful, kind and understanding. Do not rush the borrower(s) in any way. Some people like to spend a moment or two finding out who you are, others will want to make a pot of coffee, and others will be eager to get this all over with. Adjust your actions according to the personality and demands of the borrower(s). This will ease their stress level, cause them to trust you and result in a more successful signing appointment for you as well as the borrower(s).

After the borrower(s) have directed you to the area they have reserved for the signing (normally the kitchen table), ask them to supply you with a copy of their driver's license or picture ID before sitting down. This way the borrower(s) will not have to leave the table once the signing has begun.

Open up the package containing the documents for the signing. Do not remove the extra set of copies from your brief case at this point because you don't want to mix them up with any originals. Thumb through the documents and find the EXACT way the borrower(s) name is typed on the loan documents. Show the borrower(s) the way their name is typed and inform them that they need to sign ALL documents the same way. For instance, if the name on the loan document is Tammy Freck, the borrower needs to sign ALL the documents "Tammy Freck," not "T. Freck" or "Tamara Leonard-Freck" or any other variation.

Next, starting at the top of the stack of documents, identify the line where the borrower(s) are to sign and hand it to them for their signature. If there are two borrower(s), make sure both sign and hand back to you. In addition, the borrower(s) need to write in the date they are signing the document and it must be the same date typed on the documents. Review the document to make sure the borrower(s) have signed them correctly. If the document needs to be notarized, go ahead and do this at that time.

When convinced the document is correctly signed and/or notarized, turn it face down on the stack and move onto the second document. Continue in this manner until all documents have been processed and properly signed and/or notarized.

When finished, gather up the documents and place them back into your brief case or the envelope they came in. Hand the borrower(s) their set of copies, thank them for their time, wish them the best of success on their new loan and leave. The whole process should not take more than 30 minutes, but some have lasted as long as two hours depending on the amount of documents that need signed and how long the borrower(s) take to review the documents.

Is My Job Over Now?

No, your job is not over at this point. After you go back to your office you need to sit down and go through the documents one last time. Make sure they are properly signed in the right place and all pages needing a notarization have been completed. I have been known to make a mistake like forgetting to enter my

"Commission Expiration Date" and catch it during this final review stage. This step is extremely important because if you make an error, it could mean that you don't get paid. We are all humans. We have to accept the fact that we make hundreds of mistakes every single day. The difference between someone who doesn't make mistakes and one who does, is simply the fact that the person who doesn't make mistakes will double and triple-check their work and catch all their errors before anyone else does.

The next step is to notify the lender that the signing has been completed. Each lender will have a preferred method they want you to use and will provide you with a set of instructions to follow. A majority of lenders will ask you to fax them a copy of the signed HUD Settlement Statement prior to mailing the overnight package back to them. Whichever method the lender asks you to do, this step should be completed within three hours after the signing appointment is over.

Next, you will need to prepare an invoice for the company that hired you so you can get paid. Every company has a different procedure for payment, so find out what it is. Some companies have you send an invoice back to them with the loan documents and others have you fax it to a person in the accounting department. Your invoice should include the following information:

▶ Borrower(s) Names;
▶ Property Address;
▶ Lender's File Number (if applicable);

▶ Date of Signing;
▶ How documents were mailed to lender (Fed-X, UPS, etc.);
▶ Tracking Number (located on Fed-X or UPS shipping label);
▶ Name and Address of the company the documents were mailed to; and
▶ Your fee for the signing.

Of course, you should make up your invoice before you mail the documents back to the company so you will have record of all the borrower(s) information. Just keep in mind that the documents need to be mailed the SAME day the signing is done. Or, if you must do a signing in the evening (after 6:00 pm), the documents need to be mailed BEFORE NOON the next day.

Keeping Track of Invoices Due You

Make yourself an "Outstanding Invoice" list and store this file on your computer. Using your word processing software, type the name of the company, the date you completed the signing and the amount the company owes you. When they send you a check, you can remove the entry from your "Outstanding Invoice" list. This is a simple, yet "1970s method" of keeping track of which companies owe you money and you can make sure you are paid correctly.

If any company does not pay you within 30 days after you have completed the signing, contact them for an update as to when to expect your payment. Although I have never had any trouble getting paid, many NSAs have been "ripped off." The only solution I know to this problem is never to accept any more assignments from the company or file a Complaint against them in municipal court.

Or, you may be interested in the software program developed by Gabi Rekasi called My Mobile Notary. This hard-to-find software program is available at http://www.thefelicita.com/ and it is truly excellent!

After placing the mortgage documents in the Fed-X or UPS Overnight mail, your assignment is technically over, but you should always follow-up a week or so after you mailed the documents. Many companies get hurt financially by notaries because some notaries often return documents to them incomplete. When this happens the mortgage company normally has to go through the expense of drawing up new documents with a new closing date and assign another notary to complete the signing process. Often when this happens, the notary who did the incomplete work is not paid — so the tip below is one way to make sure this doesn't happen to you.

Follow-Up Tip

Once you have completed your first assignment for a company, make sure you follow-up with a telephone call to be sure all the mortgage documents were received and if you did your job correctly. The first person to contact to find out this information would be the name of the person who called and gave you the assignment in the first place. This person's name should also appear on the Confirmation Sheet you received when you

accepted the assignment. If this person does not know
if the documents were finalized properly, then call the
mortgage or title company (where you mailed the
documents back to) in order to obtain the information.

Your purpose in doing this is to find out if you did
your job properly. You also want to know if the company has any suggestions for improving your skills so
you can do a better job for them next time. You also
want to find out if the documents were processed on
time and not delayed because of your error so you can
be assured of getting paid.

You will find that not all companies operate with the
same procedures. A procedure you are required to
perform for one company may not work with another.
Therefore, it is important to know each company's
procedures and keep notes of this information in each
company's file folder. Mistakes you make may not be
notarial mistakes, but company procedural mistakes.
Don't be embarrassed if this happens. It has happened
to every NSA at least once. Just find out what you did
wrong and correct the problem the next time you conduct a signing for this company — or offer to do the job
over again free of charge to correct your mistake.
Companies will be happy to know you care about the
quality of your work and your name will move up their
list of contacts to call for future work.

The Mortgage Documents

As previously stated, not all documents will be the
same for every loan signing. That is because there are

different types of mortgage loans. However, the following list will provide you with information on most of the major documents and the basic information you need to know to process each one. Be aware that this information is not extensive and if you decide to take the plunge and become a "Certified" NSA, you will study these documents (and more) in greater depth in the NNA certification training materials.

The Note

The Note is also referred to as the "Agreement" by some companies. It is the basic contract between the borrower(s) and the lender and contains basic terms and conditions. The most important information you need to pay attention to is:

▶ The rate;
▶ Prepayment terms;
▶ Amount of principal and interest [does not include tax and insurance];
▶ What day of the month the payments are due on;
▶ Penalties for late payment; and,
▶ The amount of the loan.

The Note may also include a document entitled "Adjustable Rate Notes" which is information concerning the interest rate and how it can fluctuate.

The Deed of Trust

This document is filed in the County Recorder's Office so be very careful about making sure it is signed and notarized properly. County Recorder's can be picky people. They would just as soon deny the filing than accept it because it doesn't matter to them either way. In fact, some County Recorder's will deny a filing simply because the notary seal is not perfectly affixed and readable. Make sure you take great care to get this document perfect!

The Deed of Trust contains the following information:

▶ The loan amount;
▶ The name and address of the lender;
▶ Name(s) of the borrower(s);
▶ Location and property description;
▶ The date the loan matures;
▶ Name(s) of the Testors and Trustees;
▶ A statement that the loan is secured by the property; and
▶ An Exhibit with a property description.

The Deed of Trust also explains to the borrower(s) that they are responsible for paying taxes, principle, interest, late charges, etc. In addition, a Deed a Trust can be as few as two pages or as many as twenty pages. It is important to get the borrower(s) to initial every page of this document in the BOTTOM RIGHT HAND CORNER (front and back if document is printed on both sides).

The "Right to Cancel" Form

This document is for the benefit of the borrower(s). It allows them a minimum of three days to cancel the transaction (called a "recession period"). These three days are not always calendar days. You skip Sundays and Federal Holidays when calculating the three day "recession period." For instance, if you conducted a signing on Friday, you would count Saturday, Monday and Tuesday as the three days. If Monday happens to be a holiday, you would skip that day, making the recession period ending on Wednesday instead of Tuesday.

There are TWO places on the "Right to Cancel" form for the borrower(s) to sign. Make sure they sign the BOTTOM line and not the section indicating they wish to cancel. For beginners, this can be a tricky document, so make sure you read it carefully to ensure the borrower(s) sign on the correct signature line and do not cancel the transaction by mistake.

If the borrower(s) make a mistake and accidentally signs on the wrong signature line, the best thing to do is get a fresh copy from the extra copies you brought with you. Then, you can give the borrower(s) the copy that was mistakenly signed in the wrong place since the borrower(s) copy is not returned to the mortgage company.

QUICK TIP

If you are conducting a signing for DiTech Mortgage Company, they have nine copies of the Right to Cancel form. The forms are normally marked "Borrower(s)'s Copies" and "Lender's Copies." Make sure you have the "Lender's Copies" signed accurately and leave the "Borrower(s)'s Copies" with the borrower(s) when you leave the appointment.

The Truth in Lending Disclosure

This document will sometimes delay a signing because it contains the APR (Annual Percentage Rate) figure and many borrower(s) are confused about it. The APR is always different from the actual percentage rate because it is based on a calculation of the total amount financed and all the interest payments spanning the life of the loan.

The Truth in Lending Disclosure also includes information about what dates the monthly payment is due and the amount of the payment. As long as this figure matches what was quoted to the borrower(s), they will normally be more content in understanding why the APR is different.

HUD Settlement Statement

I mentioned this document earlier. It is the document that is normally faxed to you at the last minute or on the morning of the signing. This document is extremely important. The loan CANNOT close without it, so make sure you have received it before you leave for the signing appointment.

The HUD Settlement Statement contains information about fees and payoffs. It also contains the appraisal fee. If the borrower(s) have already paid an appraisal fee out of their pocket, and the fee is being charged again on the HUD Settlement Statement, have the borrower(s) contact the lender immediately. If the lender is not available, direct the borrower(s) to contact the lender the next business day. As previously discussed, for a refinance, the borrower(s) have three days to cancel the loan if this situation is not resolved to their satisfaction.

W9 Tax Form

The purpose of the W9 Tax Form is to enable the borrower(s) to claim mortgage interest as a tax deduction. It is also used after the loan for reference by the lender to verify the borrower(s) information.

The name of the taxpayer will appear at the top of the form and the borrower(s) will sign their name in the MIDDLE portion of the document. Normally there is one W9 Tax Form for each borrower(s), but sometimes both names can appear. If this is the case, have both borrower(s) sign on the same line in the MIDDLE portion of the document. They may have to write small to make room for both signatures because this is often a tight area on the form.

Request for Copy of Transcript of Tax Form 4506

This form allows the lender to verify the income of the borrower(s) and how much they pay in income taxes. For a husband and wife, the first 4506 Form is normally for the husband to sign and the wife signs on the "spouse" line. The name of the borrower(s) appear at the top of the document, not in the signature section.

The Uniform Residential Loan Application
Form 1003

This document often contains incorrect information, however, this document is not considered to be final. In fact this document may contain wrong birthdates or different loan amounts. If the borrower(s) are irritated by the information on this document, refer them to The Note, which contains the final and actual information.

There are different formats to follow for Form 1003, but normally the borrower(s) will initial the BOTTOM RIGHT-HAND of each page (back side if printed two-sided). Remember to have the borrower(s) sign their initials in a consistent manner within the loan documents themselves. For instance, if the borrower's name is James H. Smith, he will initial "JHS" not "JS."

Occupancy Affidavit

The purpose of this document is for the borrower(s) to state they occupy the property they are obtaining a mortgage for. In addition, the Occupancy Affidavit may ask the borrower(s) to state they have not experienced a recent loss of job, filed bankruptcy or any other sudden financial change. This document is normally notarized but they vary from lender to lender.

Errors and Omissions

This document allows the lender to correct mistakes on any loan documents. Because mistakes happen all the time, it is not unusual for documents to contain an omission of information or a typographical error. The Errors and Omission document allows the lender to correct these. This does NOT mean the lender will alter the terms of the loan — only correct errors to meet the legal requirements of the state.

The Correction Agreement with Limited Power of Attorney

Some borrower(s) think that this document gives Power of Attorney to the lender to make major changes to their loan documents. This is not the case. Instead, its purpose is to correct clerical errors like misspellings and other simple errors. It does not affect the numbers or the terms of the loan in any way.

Prepayment Rider

This document may or may not be a part of the loan package. The purpose of the Prepayment Rider is to state the penalty (if any) if the loan is repaid before the end of the term. For instance, some people can afford to make two mortgage payments per month, reducing their loan term from 30 years to 15 years but in most cases there will be a penalty for paying the loan off early during the first few years of the loan term. The borrower(s) should have already discussed this with the mortgage company before the signing appointment, so they should be familiar with the information on this document already.

The "Good Faith" Estimate

Lenders are required to give the borrower(s) an estimate of the amounts and types of costs they can expect to pay for their loan as well as the costs to close the loan. The estimated costs must be "close to" the actual charges, which is why this document is titled an "estimate." This estimate must be provided to the borrower(s) within three business days after the application for credit. The Good Faith Estimate has also been called a "pre-HUD Settlement Statement." Although it contains estimated fees, the actual HUD Settlement Statement will contain the actual fees.

Signature Affidavit

This document provides a sample of the borrower(s) signature for identification purposes. Be very careful to review the names of the borrower(s) at the top of this document. It was prepared by data entry clerks who obtained the information from a credit report. The name may not always be correct, but have the borrower(s) sign the Signature Affidavit EXACTLY as it was typed by the data entry clerk. Normally this document is notarized.

Identity Statement

Most lenders will include a document you are required to fill out that identifies the borrower(s). It will contain a place to print the borrower(s) driver's license number, date of birth, issue date of license, expiration, etc. Make sure you use the actual driver's license to record this information and do not rely on the borrower(s) to provide you with the information alone.

While you are copying the information from the driver's license or picture ID, glance at the photo to make sure it is the borrower(s). Believe it or not, fraud has been committed when a person will have a "fake" husband or wife appear at the signing. One reason this is done by a spouse is so they can obtain a mortgage on a house jointly owned by their "real" spouse without their knowledge. This of course is against the law and as a notary, you could be fined or even serve jail time if convicted.

The Identity Statement is always notarized. If the lender does not provide a place for the notary signature you can either attach a "loose certificate" (available through any notary supply company) or write in the correct notary wording for your state. To help you identify the correct wording, look at other documents requiring notarization within the loan package. Each state is different, but just to help you recognize the type of wording I am referring to, here is a sample for the state of Ohio:

State of **Ohio**   : **ss.**
County of **Franklin**   :

Sworn to and subscribed before me this ____ day of _____, 2004.

_____

Notary Signature   (SEAL)
My Commission Expires: _____

Statement of Information

This document takes about ten minutes to complete. Some notaries prefer to fill out this document first and then insert it back into its proper order. The Statement of Information normally asks for personal information from the borrower(s) such as the state they were born in, employment history, history of previous addresses, prior marriages, names of children, etc.

Automatic Payment Document

If the borrower(s) wish to have their mortgage payment automatically deducted from their bank account each month, they will need to sign this document. Also, they need to provide you with a VOIDED check or deposit slip from the bank account where they want their payments automatically deducted. Staple this VOIDED check or deposit slip to the Automatic Payment Document so it doesn't get lost.

Check Disbursement

As previously mentioned, you may encounter a situation where you are required to collect money from the borrower(s) after the signing is complete. (This information can be found on Lines 303, 1601 or 1604 of the HUD Settlement Statement). But this is not the norm and often times we get in a hurry and forget about checking the HUD.

In most cases, the borrower(s) will be receiving money back from the lender when the loan closes. In these cases, the lender will not release the check to the borrower(s) until after the three day recession period has expired. Lenders do not want to risk the chance of issuing a check and then having the loan be canceled by the borrower(s) within three days. Therefore, you will never be delivering funds to borrower(s) but you may have to collect them.

If the lender asks you to collect a cashier's check, a certified check or a money order from the borrower(s) at the signing appointment, make sure you have discussed this with the borrower(s) PRIOR to the appointment. This way the borrower(s) have time to obtain the check from their bank made payable to the mortgage company. Attach this check (I prefer to staple) on top of the loan package so the lender will spot it immediately after opening the package you mail back to them.

Journal Entries

Most states require a notary public to keep a journal that provides details of every document they notarize during the course of their careers. For Ohio, as well as a few other states, a notary journal is not required except for certain documents that are rarely encountered by most notaries. However, if you are a notary in a state that requires you to keep a journal — do not leave the borrower(s) home until you have made the entry and had them sign your journal. Also, some states now require you to make a thumbprint of the borrower(s). Check with your state, the National Notary Association or another notary in your area to find out the proper procedures.

Become a "Certified" NSA

Because each lender is different and each loan is unique, I am unable to list every single type of document you will encounter. To further your education, I strongly urge you to enroll in the Certified Signing Agent training course developed and administered by the National Notary Association. The course taught me excellent skills as well as being an interesting read.

Becoming a Certified Signing Agent has many advantages. It will normally give you an "edge" over non-certified notaries and in most cases you are paid 25% more per signing because of your advanced training. In addition you receive a really nice 8x10 Certificate of Completion and your name is printed in the National Notary Association magazine. To obtain the materials or find out more about the course, go online to http://www.signingagent.com/infotraining.cfm.

Notary Errors and Omission Insurance

It is also a good idea for every NSA to obtain an Errors and Omission Insurance policy. This will protect you in case you make notarial errors that result in a legal proceeding. Some states will require all notaries to do this, while other states make it optional. I found the best rate for my Errors and Omission Insurance through the National Notary Association. As a member of the NNA I only paid $32 for a two year policy with a $15,000 liability limit. The policy is through the Western Surety Company, a well-known and respected insurance company.

Paying Taxes on the Money
You Earn as a NSA

Every mortgage, title or signing company you accept a signing appointment from will ask you to fill out a Form W9, "Request for Taxpayer Identification Number and Certification." To view and print out the form for your records, go online to http://www.irs.gov/pub/irs-pdf/fw9.pdf. The document is in PDF format so make sure you have Adobe Acrobat Reader installed. If you don't have Acrobat, go to http://www.adobe.com/products/acrobat/readstep.html to download a free copy and install it. You will need Adobe Acrobat anyway if you accept loan documents by email in PDF format.

The purpose of the W9 Form is to pay you for your notary services and issue a 1099-Form at the end of the year. Since no taxes are deducted from your NSA income, you will be responsible for paying the taxes on the money you earn. Depending on the income taxes you have already paid from other employment throughout the year, your NSA income may or may not raise your taxes — but it is still required to be reported as additional income and must be listed on your tax return.

For me, I fill out a Form-1040 tax return and include a Schedule C-EZ reflecting the total amount of income I earned that was not taxed. This figure is then transferred over to the proper line on Form-1040. If you hire a tax preparer to complete your tax return, you don't need to worry much about it. But I prefer to do my own taxes so I have knowledge of exactly what is going on. If I have a question, I call the IRS. Contrary to popular belief, the people at the IRS are kind and patient folks. The IRS agents I have spoken to have taken a great deal of time educating me in properly completing my own tax return. The telephone number to your IRS office should appear on the back of your tax booklet.

Now that we have covered almost everything you need to know in order to do your job as a NSA, you are now ready to set up your NSA business and start earning money. We will cover these topics in the sections to follow.

Setting Up Your NSA Business

*Understanding is a wellspring of life unto him that
hath it: but the instruction of fools is folly.*

Proverbs 16:22

The Truth Behind the Three "Myths" of Starting a Business

Regardless of what you have heard on television, managing and operating your own small business is hard work. On television you will hear success stories of people who opened a business one day, made $10,000 their first month — and now they get to spend time with their family, take exotic vacations and do whatever they want. This is a total misconception!

Although running a small part-time business as a NSA is not very difficult, if you choose to work at home full-time, you will find yourself working harder compared to working for an employer. Sure, there are days that I can take off work, but I have to replace that time working a 12-16 hour day to make up for the time I took off. That doesn't happen when you work for an employer. If you are sick and have to take a day off, you normally get paid. Although your work may pile up while you are off sick, you are normally still in a position to leave at the end of your work day. But if you were running your own business, you may have to be available 24 hours a day for emergencies and you will not be able to call in sick.

Remember when you first started seeking employment back in your early teenage years? You probably accepted any job that anyone offered. You knew you did not have work experience so you could not afford to be picky and choosy. The only purpose you had in mind at that time was making money – not building a career in a particular industry.

However, after gaining a few years of experience under your belt – you probably started seeking employment with companies who offered a good salary or good benefits. At this point, you could afford to be a bit more choosy because you had something of value to bargain with – your previous experience. So you looked around and found a job that not only made you happy and fulfilled, but also met your personal financial needs.

Unfortunately though, when someone with no previous business experience decides to start their first business, they revert back to their "teenage" days. They are enticed by the leer of easy money and less work. They don't seem to care what they are doing to earn this extra money (within reason of course) – they are only focusing on the plus side of the small business myths they have head about, which are: (1) You get to be your own boss; (2) You get to set your own hours; and (3) You work less but make more money. Let's look at each one of these "myths" individually and learn the truth behind them.

Myth No. 1: You Get to Be Your Own Boss

Yes, it's true that you are your own boss when you own a small business, but your power is only limited to your small environment; such as your office staff if you are fortunate enough to have one. That is because your customers now become your boss and you have to serve your customers BETTER than you probably serve the boss where you are (or were) employed. However, if you want to use the title of "boss" and make your ego swell – that's something you will have to decide for yourself. But remember that no matter what position you hold in life – there is always someone higher up on the ladder than you are and always will be. Whether it be customers or employers – you will always have someone to answer to – so get used to it now.

Myth No. 2: You Get to Set Your Own Hours

The myth that owning a business allows you to set your own hours is really a myth. Although you may not have to be tied to a clock (like you are with an employer), you still must meet deadlines, adhere to the schedules of your customers and work a lot of times when you really don't want to. If you are sick and emergency work needs done, you will have to do the work or pay someone else to help you. Have you ever saw the sign that says: "The buck stops here"? This becomes your motto when you own a business and you will assume responsibility for everything.

Myth No. 3: You Work Less but Make More Money

Talk to any successful small business owner and you will find this myth is missing a big element of truth. That truth is: "In order to make more money, you have to work very, very, hard." Owning your own business is not the "chocolate cake and icing" that many idea marketers picture it to be. For instance: You can definitely make more money owning your own business but you will be working many more hours to earn that money. As a small business owner, I can tell you that I worked 7 days a week, 12 hours or more every day, for a period of two years when I started my business. Sure, I made great money – but I worked for every dime I earned.

However, after a few years of building your business, you may reach a point where everything is running smooth and you can afford to take some time off. You also may be able to be more flexible with your working hours and spend more time with the family. But these benefits do not exist until you have put in a lot of hard work and built a successful business. This is one reason why many people fail in business. They do not have the patience to wait on the benefits so they just quit. Then they will go work a year or more for an employer to get the employer-paid benefits. If people have the patience to wait on employer-paid benefits – why don't they have the same patience when it comes to building their own business?

Perhaps the answer to this question lies in the fact that working for an employer and running your own business are two totally different things. The main differences are:

▶ You do not receive a steady paycheck when you own your own business. When you work for an employer you do.

▶ As a business owner, you will be on call 24-hours a day. If an emergency should arise, you will need to handle the problem. If you work for an employer – they handle emergency problems and you normally get to stay home if it is your day off.

▶ You do not get paid vacations, sick leave or medical benefits if you are a business owner. If you are sick one day, it will be your responsibility to see the jobs are completed and finished on time regardless of how you feel. When you work for an employer you normally receive sick time, vacations and medical benefits. Also, you do not have to be as concerned about deadlines because co-workers can be used as a back up if you are unavailable.

Medical Benefits for the Self-Employed

I have spoken with many freelancers and one of the biggest concerns they had about going full-time with their own business was giving up their health insurance. Unless your spouse has insurance to cover you at their place of employment – you will be on your own.

However, as more and more people become self-employed, the insurance companies are beginning to take notice. Anthem Insurance (located online at http://www.anthem.com) is one health insurance provider that offers individual health insurance at reasonable rates. I contacted them to get some quotes and was quoted $172.57 per month with a $500 deductible. I am sure these rates will change by the time this book is printed, but Anthem is one company worth checking into when searching for individual health insurance.

Or, you can use the method I use and that is not to have any health insurance at all. Although I am a diabetic, I eat right, stay healthy and exercise daily. If I get a cold or flu, I take care of it myself with herbal remedies. I go to the doctor every three months and have blood tests run every six months to monitor my sugar levels. My doctor knows that I do not have insurance so he charges me $45 per office visit. Besides, if I had insurance, the doctor would submit a bill to the insurance company, wait for months to receive his payment and then maybe only receive a portion of what he submitted (in some cases $45 or less).

For my medications, I use a Canadian pharmacy to fill my prescriptions. For instance, if I have my prescriptions filled at a local pharmacy it would cost me $450 per month. However, by purchasing the same medication from the Canadian pharmacy I only pay $80 per month. That's a huge savings!

But what would happen if an emergency occurred like a heart attack or other threatening condition? All hospitals have payment plans to help you pay back the bill. First you meet with the hospital's accounting department and get the bill reduced since you do not have insurance. Then you pay the balance off over time without any interest charges.

Managing Your Business

When I started my first business (Graphico Publishing) back in October of 1988, I "thought" I knew what I was doing. However, I quickly learned that I was "dumb as a box of rocks" when it came to managing a business. This is one reason why people fail when they start a small business — they have absolutely no concept of what managing a business is all about. But it is not entirely their fault. Most people have spent their lives working for someone else and have no experience in this area. There is nothing wrong with admitting you are as "dumb" as I used to be. The main issue is whether you will open yourself to education, or sit back, make excuses and feel sorry for yourself; thereby stunting the growth and success of your business.

The best way to learn about managing a business is to seek out people who are already successful in running a small business. How do you do this? The internet has made it simple. Go to any search engine and type in the words "small business." You'll find a ton of links to start sifting through. A few good places I recommend you start are:

- ▶ http://www.businesstown.com/
- ▶ http://www.isquare.com/
- ▶ http://www.powerhomebiz.com/
- ▶ http://www.businessownersideacafe.com/
- ▶ http://www.businessnation.com/
- ▶ http://www.allfreelance.com/start.html
- ▶ http://www.workathome-com.com/
- ▶ http://www.entrepreneur.com/

Join a free discussion group (available at Yahoo, MSN and thousands more) and read and study the materials available to you on the internet. You will learn that if you surround yourself with the knowledge of people who are more successful than you are, you will be successful also.

Business Planning

When I started my first business I immediately started looking for ways to make money. I thought it would be a waste of time for me to write a business plan or think about any long-range plans. At that time, I had no idea what direction my business was going so how could I plan anything? But that was where I made my first mistake (not knowing where by business was going) and I hope I can save some of you from making the same mistake.

Let's look at a "real life" scenario: If you are sitting on the couch watching television and you want a can of Pepsi that is in the refrigerator, you know that in order to get that Pepsi, you will have to get up from the couch and walk into the kitchen, open up the refrigerator door, get your can of Pepsi and walk back to the couch and sit down. You formed the plan in your mind of how to get the Pepsi immediately after you first decided you wanted one. Normally we do not think of something this simple as requiring a plan because we do it millions of times without much thought. However, we used short-term planning techniques and achieved our goal of getting the can of Pepsi in the refrigerator.

As a newly formed business, you may not have the experience yet to complete long-range plans; but you should be able to set some short-term plans. These plans first begin with a "vision" (just like you first decided you wanted a can of Pepsi while you were still sitting on the couch). Next, you need to plan some ideas out in your head of how you are going to accomplish that vision. There are no step-by-step rules for accomplishing this because every business is different; but your short-term plans should include (at a bare minimum) information such as:

▶ A description of your business in 25 words or less;

▶ Variety of plans you intend to use in order to achieve your business vision; and

▶ List of equipment or products you need to purchase in order to grow your business.

Setting an Advertising Budget

When you start a new business you may be excited and want to start investing in advertising right away. But before you spend one dime, you need to review your finances to determine how much money you can afford to spend for advertising. Write down how much income you receive per month. Subtract your housing costs, food, clothing, medical, insurance, automobile and other personal expenses. The remaining figure is how much you have left to dedicate toward growing your business. For some people — they may have no money to invest into advertising. That's because some people start their first business with the conception they will make money first and use that money to grow their business. Unfortunately, this is a bad decision. I know, because I made the mistake myself.

Let me give you another "real life" example. When I started my first business I had absolutely no money. I

had been laid off my job and was existing on unemployment — and my unemployment was getting ready to
run out. I was in a desperate situation financially and I
was stupid enough to start a business at that time. If I
could go back in time, I would have advised myself to
work for an employer and build up a "nest-egg" first.
Starting a business without some "nest-egg" is the
same thing as a teenager moving out to their first
apartment with no savings. Teenagers who do this
either end up moving back in with mom and dad or
struggling for many months. The same effect will occur
if you start a business with no money.

On the other hand, I had a friend who also started a
business at the same time I did. But she was married
and her husband paid all the bills until she got her
business up and rolling. Every dime my friend made
with her business she was able to invest 100% back
into building her company. Within less than one year
she was making $5,000 per month and after three years
her business was making an average of $150,000 per
year. This could not have been achieved if my friend
had used all her business income to pay personal overhead expenses and not invest any money back into her
business for advertising and marketing.

Make a Daily Work Plan

Even if you have no income coming in at the present
time with your business, you still should write out a
work plan for each day. Before you go to bed at night,
write out a plan of what you need to do the next day.
Some of these plans for a NSA might be signing up with

a new mortgage company, researching notary job links
on the web to find signing companies, designing your
website, signing up for a marketing class, etc.

Set Up a Good Calendar System

Many notaries prefer to use PIMs (personal information managers) to keep track of appointments and "to-
do" lists. This way, they can take their PIM with them
wherever they go and quickly refer to it. You can either
pick up an appointment book at your local office supply
store, or purchase a computerized PIM.

Another great calendar system is offered by Yahoo
online at http://calendar.yahoo.com. The advantage to
using Yahoo's calendar is that your information can be
accessed from any computer. You can store information
on contacts, calendar items, to-do lists, and even re-
minders that will send you emails to nag you when
items are coming due.

Develop Good Organizational Skills

Having excellent organizational skills is the best way
to avoid most problems working as an NSA. First of all
you must understand the extreme importance of the
documents entrusted to you. Once these documents are
executed, the lives of the borrower(s) will be changed
for many years. A mistake could cost the lender a loan,
the borrower(s) may lose the keys on a newly purchased home or unnecessary money may need to be
spent by the borrower(s) to correct the documents for a
second signing since additional fees may be involved.

These are just a few of the reasons why your job as a NSA carries such great importance in the loan process. Therefore, it is essential you have good organizational skills in order to succeed in this business.

Develop a Good Filing System

Even if you have not made any money yet, you still need to establish some sort of filing system and organize the way you plan to do things. This way, when you get busy your filing system will already be set up and in place to help you maintain a smooth operation.

Your filing system should be set up in a way that works for you. Every business owner has their own filing system and you will have your own way of doing things also. But all too often people think that everything needs to be saved because they are sure it will be needed the minute after it is tossed away. This is why filing systems end up growing to the point where a entire storage room is needed to handle the clutter. And when you filing gets this far out of hand — you will never be able to find anything when you need it.

To prevent this from happening, every time a piece of paper crosses your desk make the decision to do one of the following:

▶ Toss it because you can always find the information online if you need it in again the future.

▶ Toss it but retain any contact information in your roladex for future reference.

▶ Scan it into an electronic file for easy storage on a diskette or CD-Rom.

▶ Keep in a place you can easily find it.

You may want to start by keeping four file folders on your desk. Label them: (1) Top Priority; (2) Current Projects; (3) To Be Filed, and (4) To Do Later. As you process each piece of paper within the file folders you can then make the decision to toss, scan or file the paper in another folder for future use as covered above. This should help you get off to a good start.

The Importance of Minimizing Mistakes

Another important subject that some people tend to overlook when they are running a small business are developing skills to minimize mistakes. First, you have to accept the fact that you and everyone else in the world make hundreds of mistakes every day. This is the price we have to pay for being human, so accept it. Double and triple-checking everything you do is the best way to minimize mistakes. However, most people get in a hurry and skip over this crucial step. They do not conceive how a simple mistake can be that big of a deal — but let me give you a scenario to think about:

A successful small businessman named Bobby needed to purchase 25 computer systems for an upcoming sale he was having. He had just attended an open house of computer suppliers and met a lady named Shelley who owned a computer warehouse. Shelley had some excellent prices and Bobby decided to order

$3,000 worth of merchandise from her for his upcoming sale. Not only was he getting a good deal and would make a great profit from the sale, he also wanted to establish a possible long-term business relationship with Shelley so he could obtain future merchandise at a substantial cost savings.

Bobby ordered the merchandise and paid Shelley's company with a $3,000 check. When the check arrived at the bank to be cashed, the bank teller accidentally keyed in the wrong account number. The account number the bank teller keyed in did not have sufficient funds to pay the $3,000 check and the check automatically bounced. It was returned to Shelley marked "NSF" which means "non-sufficient funds."

Although the bank accepted full responsibility for their mistake, the repercussions this simple error (keying in ONE wrong digit) caused to many people was not able to be corrected. First, Bobby did not receive the merchandise in time for his sale. This caused Bobby to lose about $12,000 in anticipated profit he would have made. Secondly, the business relationship Bobby had attempted to establish with Shelley was now dissolved. Even though Shelley eventually learned that Bobby was totally innocent in the matter, she was still hesitant about accepting another order from him. It would take Bobby several months, if not years to generate the trust he lost from this simple clerical error and obtain the merchandise discounts he had originally hoped to achieve.

As you can see — simple, tiny, little errors can cause effects on some, many or masses of people. Unfortu-

nately, I have encountered many people today who do
not think far enough ahead to anticipate how a simple
mistake they make can have such extreme effects. I
can only hope that the information I just provided will
cause you to think differently. Force yourself to double
and triple-check your work. And if you do make a
mistake, don't show yourself to be inexperienced and
"dumb" by trying to make excuses for your error. Instead, just say *"I am sorry. What can I do to fix the
problem?"* Then, fix the problem and move on with life.
All too often I watch people make excuses for their
behavior instead of just accepting facts, solving the
problem and going forward. Excuses are meant to cover
up mistakes — not correct them. In fact, making excuses is the same thing as trying to put a band-aid on a
poisonous snake bite. This will never cure or correct the
problem. Instead, you will waste time and money on
the band-aid.

I was sitting in a room full of attorney's one day and
I said, *"Why is it so hard to admit you made a mistake?
Isn't it easier to just admit it then to spend so much
time coming up with an excuse as to why you made the
mistake in the first place?"* I was shocked when two of
the attorneys overhead me and said in unison – *"That
may be true, except I don't make mistakes."* Everyone
else in the room laughed, but it shows you how egotisti-
cal human nature is. So try to understand that everyone on the planet makes many mistakes on a daily
basis. (I know I make them so I have to develop ways
to constantly check myself so I minimize my mistakes).
When you make a mistake and are confronted about it –
just apologize and ask what you need to do to correct

the problem. People will become sympathetic and understanding when you take this approach. However, if you start coming up with a list of excuses as to why you made the mistake – you are not correcting the problem and the impression you make on the other person will be negative.

Should You Own Your Own Business or Work for Someone Else?

Many of the people reading this book will be people who have never owned and operated their own business before. You may be a person who has always worked for someone else and you have no idea what owning a business is like. Or, maybe you have started your first business and are still in the "honeymoon" stage where you think you will become financially successful in a short period of time. Or perhaps you are a notary who used to make good money doing closings (because you entered the field when the interest rates were low) but now find that your income has dropped considerably. Believe me – I understand how people in all these stages of business think. I was right where you are many times during the course of my career.

Starting a business is kind of like raising a child. You have to give an infant and toddler a lot of attention and training. But when that child grows up and becomes a successful doctor, all the hard work and time you invested in your child is rewarded. That's the same way you have to think about starting a business.

However, if you do not have this determination and drive at this time in your life, or feel you would be more

comfortable working for someone else, get a part-time
or full-time job in the real estate industry. Employers
capable of teaching you a great deal about the real
estate market in order to further your NSA career would
be: (1) real estate attorneys; (2) mortgage/title companies; and (3) real estate agents just to name a few.
While you are working for these types of employers –
absorb every piece of knowledge you can from the
experts because everything you learn from them will
aide in the success of your own business.

If you are a paralegal, it should be easy for you to
find additional part-time work with a real estate attorney in your area before starting a NSA business. When I
used to work in litigation, I found a job working for a
real estate attorney on the weekends. I worked four
hours a day on Saturday preparing deeds, typing property descriptions and ordering title searches. I made an
extra $50 a week and gained an excellent education
about the real estate process that helped me tremen-
dously as a NSA.

If you have been a NSA for over a year or so and
you do several closings per month for mortgage companies, you may have found that your income has recently
dropped or is inconsistent. I get this question all the
time from other notaries. They want to know why they
are no longer getting the amount of signings they used
to get. Notaries who ask these questions are experienced NSA's and are probably at a stage where they
need to incorporate more notary services into their
business to expand. NSA's in this category will love
Section 4 of this book which begins on Page 95.

Remember, the real estate industry is NOT a market that remains steady at all times. Look at how the stock market fluctuates from minute to minute. That is because the stock market is based upon the buying trends of people – and we all know that people are unpredictable. The real estate market is also based on the buying trends of people – and it will be constantly changing.

Following these suggestions will help you to learn the real estate industry from the inside out. Then after a period of time, you will have the knowledge and confidence you need to open your own business and be successful. Just because you find yourself in a position where you may not be able to take on the responsibility of a business of your own at this time – that doesn't mean you won't be able to at a future date.

Setting Up Your Notary Office

The first step in increasing your income as a NSA is to set up your business and conduct it like a profes-sional. Some notaries come into this industry thinking all they have to do is take some papers to somebody's house, notarize them, stick them back in an envelope and get bunches of money without any effort. Some companies even use marketing gimmicks to entice notaries like: *"Make up to $125 per Signing"* and *"Earn*

Extra Money as a NSA." Advertising like this will help to bring "business opportunity" minded people into the industry. Business opportunity people are people who are not necessarily concerned with the quality of the job they do – but are only seeking to make extra money. If this is how you perceive the NSA business, this may be one reason why you are not getting any assignments. So if you are truly interested in building a successful business in this field, we need to work on this thinking pattern. The first step is to set up your business like a business so you will feel like you really are a business owner and conduct yourself like one.

I don't mean for you to get the "big head" and start walking around town in $1,000 suits telling people you are the world's gift to business. True business owners who become successful and run their businesses for many years are normally humble people who will "go that extra mile" to please their customer. Anyone you work for whether it is a mortgage, title or signing company becomes YOUR customer and they need to be treated as such. Erase the mindset that you are a powerful business owner who expects the world to stop revolving when you walk into a room. This type of thinking has destroyed millions of small businesses and people wonder "why" they failed. So take a good look at yourself and work on improving your humility and personal desire for a quality product.

The Importance of Business Cards

It is essential for you to have business cards indicating you are a notary public. The lowest price I have found for business cards is through the National Notary Association but you must become a member. At the time this book was written, you can get a set of 1,000, two-color business cards from the National Notary Association for only $39.95.

Here are some other good places on the internet to purchase a set of business cards but they cost considerably more than the National Notary Association:

- ▶ http://www.vistaprint.com/
- ▶ http://www.business-cards.com/
- ▶ http://www.weprintcolor.com/
- ▶ http://www.bizcardsxpress.com/

Want more choices? Go to any search engine and type in the search words: "business cards" and have fun shopping and comparing prices.

Or, if you cannot afford to buy business cards at this time, you can improvise by going to your local office supply store (Staples, Office Max, etc.) and buy a set of blank designer business cards. A set of 250 blank sheets normally costs under $5 so anyone can afford them. Using your word processing software (such as Microsoft Word) you can type the information for your business card, place a sheet of the blank cards you purchased from the office supply store in your printer and print out a set of 10 at a time. (Business cards come 10 to a page).

Here are the step-by-step instructions for printing business cards using Microsoft Word Version 2002.

Other version upgrades should be similar.

▶ Click on the "Tools" option within MS Word.

▶ Select the "Letters and Mailings" option.

▶ Select the "Envelopes and Labels" option.

▶ A menu will pop up with two tabs. One is labeled "Envelopes" and the other is labeled "Labels." Click on the "Labels" tab and a blank screen will be shown where you begin typing your text.

▶ But before typing any text, click on the "Options" button.

▶ The Labels Options menu will appear. Look under the "Product number" area and select the label size that fits the blank business card labels you purchased from the office supply store. Most label formats are numbered with the industry standard of Avery. So if you look under "Product Number" and scroll down to the "business card" area, you will find several choices. Some of them are "5371 Business Card," "5376 Business Card" etc. These numbers (5371 and 5376) refer to the Avery product number, which should be printed on the outside of the business card labels you purchased.

▶ When you select the proper business card label to match the size of the business cards you purchased at the office supply store, the dimensions will automatically appear in the "Label Information" area. Take a standard ruler and measure one of the blank business cards to make sure the measurements match the dimensions in the "Label Information" area. If not, select another "Product Number" until you have selected the right size of business card.

▶ Now, all you have to do is click on "OK" to return to the "Envelopes and Labels" menu. Simply type in your text and print one page of business cards. Make sure you only print ONE sheet of business cards. When this page prints, remove it from your printer and inspect it. Separate one of the business cards at the perforated edge and make sure the information is lined up and laid out correctly. Adjust your text alignment if necessary and make sure the business cards are printing properly before proceeding with printing all your business cards.

▶ Use your business cards by including them in every piece of business mail you send out – including placing one in the mortgage documents you return after you complete a signing. This way, the lender knows how to contact you if a problem should come up. Although lenders will normally contact the company that hired you if there is a problem, it cannot hurt to provide them with your contact information as a back-up.

Also put a few business cards in your wallet or purse and hand them out to all business people you come into contact with. Business cards are often never thrown away and your contact information is easily accessible for others in the future. There is a whole book written about how effective business cards are to the rise or fall of a business. So even if you don't see the importance of business cards in your marketing at this time, you will soon find out when you start distributing them.

QUICK TIP

Blank business cards normally come pre-scored and 10 per page. This means you do not have to use scissors to cut the business cards apart. Instead, you just fold on the perforation and remove each card after printing. But when I only folded one time along the perforation, the edges of my business card were uneven and looked home-made. I found that when I bent the perforation in one direction, then bent it back a second time – the business card was easily removed and the edges were crisp and professional looking.

Finally, while most people know the information that should appear on a business card I want to cover it here for people who are brand new to business. This information is: (1) Your name; (2) Your address; (3) Your city, state and zip code; (4) Your telephone number; (5) Your fax number; (6) Your website address.

If you have a website, you would also include this information on your business card but you may not want to include your email address. The reason for this is because email addresses change. As a small business, it will take you some time to use 500 or 1,000 business cards. If you purchase a set with your email address on them and your email address changes — you will have to throw away the business cards you didn't use.

It is NEVER acceptable for a business person to cross out old information on a printed business card, write in the new information and give the business card to a potential client. Therefore, think about what information you know will NOT be changing so you will know what information to include on the business cards you order. Of course, if you design your own business cards with your word processing software, your can print a small quantity of business cards as you need them. Then if any information changes in the future, you can print new cards with the updated information.

I cannot stress it clearly enough – NEVER give out a business card with old information. Doing this will automatically label you as unprofessional and the quality of your work may be perceived as unorganized and questionable. Therefore, it is best to always throw old business cards away with wrong information rather than try to recycle them.

Other Basic Office Supplies

Other than business cards you also need the basic office supplies (paper, pens, binder clips, post-it notes, paper clips, etc). As a notary, you will also need a laser fax machine. This is because legal documents must be printed on a "laser" printer. A laser printer uses dry toner to print a page and an inkjet uses wet ink making it easier to forge documents. Don't make the mistake of buying one of those fax machines that prints with a ribbon. I made that mistake once and found out the refill ribbons cost over $25 and I was only able to print 50 sheets of paper before the ribbon needed replaced.

This means I was paying about 50¢ for each page printed by the fax machine.

After throwing my first "ribbon" fax machine out in the trash dumpster, I called my friend who sells printers and fax machines (which I should have done in the first place). I asked him what the most economical fax machine on the market was – as well as the best quality one. Today I use a Brother Intellifax 2800 and I highly recommend it to you. The fax machine cost me less than $200. The refill cartridges are only $22 and I get almost 3,000 printed pages from one cartridge. This means my page cost was reduced from 50¢ per page to only .0007, which is almost nothing.

Do You Really Need a Website for Marketing?

If you truly want to get "ahead of the game" and show the mortgage, title and signing companies you are serious about your job – you need a website. The web-site does not have to be elaborate. Even if it is just one page containing a copy of your resume that will be sufficient for now. However, when I mention this idea to most notaries they immediately say: *"Oh no! I can't afford that and I don't know how to make a web page."*

But the truth of the matter is – the monthly hosting fees for having a website average only $9.95 per month. Anyone can afford that — so there is no excuse for not having a website. People who have been in business for some time already know this. So when they encounter someone who does not have a website, they perceive you as a beginner since it appears you cannot afford $9.95 to have your own website.

To illustrate my point about low prices, go on the internet to Bummer Hosting (this is the company I use for the 50 State Notary website). Their website is located at www.bummerhosting.com. You will find out about all the services they provide when you decide to host your website with them. You will be amazed at the low prices and perhaps understand that having a website is not the "big deal" that you thought it was. You can also do a search on the internet using search words like "web hosting" and compare prices and features.

Securing a Domain Name

After locating a web hosting company, the next step is to secure a domain name. What does this mean? The word "domain" means the top level. The best way to illustrate this in relation to the internet is by comparing a domain name to the folders on your computer.

When you create a new MAIN folder on your computer you may name it something like "letters." Inside this folder you will probably create subfolders and call them names like "personal" and "business". This way when you type a personal letter, you would save it under the "personal" folder which is inside the main "letters" folder you first created. The "letters" folder is essentially the same thing as a domain name. It is the top-level folder name and any folders you create within it are subfolders, just like you are used to making on your own computer.

Sample URL:

http://www.50statenotary.com/directory/index.html

domain   file   page
name   name   name

The sample above is a good example of a URL (which stands for **U**niversal **R**esource **L**ocator) and how each part is broken down into individual folders (just like on your computer) which is indicated by a front slash ("/"). Have you ever heard people ask you for a URL? If so, the sample above is what they are talking about. Suppose you are visiting a website that you find interesting and want to share its contents with someone else. Simply do the following:

► Place your mouse pointer in the area of your web browser (the software you use to access the internet such as Internet Explorer, Netscape, AOL, etc.) where the entire URL appears. Click one time and the entire URL should be highlighted. If not, drag your mouse from one end (starting with the http://) and highlight the entire URL.

► Next, hold down the CTRL key on your keyboard and press the letter "C". Although you won't see any-thing happen on your computer screen, this will copy the text you have highlighted to your computer's memory clipboard so you can paste it without retyping.

► Now, prepare to send an email to the person you want to share this website with. In the text of your email, go to the point where you want the URL you copied to appear. Hold down the CTRL key on your keyboard and press the letter "V". This will paste the entire URL you just copied. When the person receives your email they can click on this link and immediately be taken to the webpage you were viewing.

QUICK TIP

NEVER try to retype an entire URL. Always copy and paste it. This will prevent you from making typographical errors and provide you with 100% assurance the URL is correct and will work for the person receiving the email. Nothing is more time-consuming or appears unprofessional than sending a link to a person and it doesn't work. By copying and pasting the URL, you will never have this problem occur.

The Importance of a Domain Name

As I briefly covered before – in order for companies to trust that you are a serious business professional, you must have a domain name established. Don't make the mistake of getting a free webpage or using the space provided by your internet service provider such as Earthlink and AOL to use for your business. These free web space pages are only designed for PERSONAL use. They should never be a substitute for a webpage you are using to market yourself to companies.

For example, have you ever seen a web address that looked something like:

http://www.topdomain.com/webpages/customers/
~patlivingston4126/index.html

I have seen web addresses like these many times and immediately I recognize the person as a beginner who is probably not very serious about their business. People obtain addresses like these because they are normally given a free web page when they sign up with an ISP for internet service. As a serious business person, I would never do business with a company who had a website domain name like this. Why? Because they will probably be out of business before they cash my check and I may never get what I paid for since they are not serious enough to register a domain name which only cost a few dollars.

A "real world" example of how an internet domain name is essential to your success as a business would be like comparing the difference between a street vendor selling jewelry to an established store like the diamond and gold company located in the mall. Who would you trust the most to provide you with a quality product? Even if you did purchase your jewelry from the street vendor, what happens if the jewelry turns out to be a piece of junk? Can you find the street vendor again and get your money back? It would be very doubtful. That is why people would prefer to deal with established businesses and the only way to prove you are an established and serious business owner is to secure a domain name for your business. There are no shortcuts.

Domain Name Ideas and Where to Get One

If you visit the main Network Solutions website at http://www.networksolutions.com, you will see they have an area on the front page of their website where you can type in a domain name and check for availability. (Other websites offer this same free service also). "Availability" means that you cannot purchase a domain name that someone else has already purchased. Just like you could not buy the domain name "50StateNotary.Com" because I already own it and have it registered. Registering an internet domain name has absolutely nothing to do with registering a business name with the government. Internet domain names are issued by one company named Network Solutions. They are not associated with any government agency and you can purchase any domain name you want as long as it is not registered to someone else. Domain names are normally purchased for a period of two years. After that, you must renew the name or someone else can purchase it.

Some internet marketers will purchase a domain name that is their own name. The first domain name I purchased was VictoriaRing.Com and it turned out to be a wise decision. This was because I had the flexibility to turn the website into anything I wanted at any future date. If I had purchased a domain name like "RingMobileNotaryServices" I would have been stuck with only providing mobile notary services. If I decided to do something else, I would have to purchase another domain name to reflect the new type of business. For example, I presently have the following domain names registered in my name:

▶ http://www.50statenotary.com
▶ http://www.victoriaringconsulting.com
▶ http://www.servantofjesuschrist.com

Each of these websites has a different theme as well as different products and services that are offered. I do not have three separate bank accounts or three separate business licenses. The URLs above are registered domain names only. Many people don't understand this. One time I mentioned in an issue of <u>The Notary News</u> (my weekly ezine for NSA's) that my 50StateNotary website was just one of my websites and that I had others also. I received some hate mail from a few notaries who said they did not want to do business with a company that was getting ready to fold up. They "assumed" that since I had other websites that 50StateNotary was going to become a non-functioning business.

Now that you have learned how domain names work, you can understand "why" this attitude was totally ridiculous. The notaries sending these hate mails not only demonstrated their lack of knowledge for basic internet skills – but they also showed their unprofessional behavior by sending hate mail. There is never a reason to send hate mail to anyone – no matter how much anger you feel. If you are this angry you should keep your mouth shut and move on with life. Traceable emails are not the place to be mean and hateful since your words are in print and can be circulated all over the world – making you look like a fool. I know this is true because back when I was a new beginner on the internet, I lost my temper one time and said some pretty rude stuff. My email was posted on the internet for almost one year and it was very embarrassing. I am thankful this occurred back in 1994 and that the web page containing my written comments no longer exists.

Another tip in selecting a domain name is not to choose one where the name is too long. Your first and last name is probably good enough — but something like "VictoriaRingNotaryServicesForTheStateofOhio" is ridiculous. You have to think about the fact that people will probably be typing your URL in their web browser to visit your website for the first time. The chances of making a typographical error when typing a domain name of this length will be very high. You will be bombarded with email messages telling you they cannot access your website. So save yourself the added grief – and choose a domain name that is short, easy to remember and not difficult to type.

Some tips to help you start thinking on the correct path in properly choosing a domain name are:

▶ gloriajoyce.com is a good domain name, but if your name is something like Maggie Catherine Meade-Snyder you can easily see that it would become maggiecatherinemeadesnyder.com for a domain name. This is hard for most people to read, let alone retype. So write out your name on a piece of paper and see how it looks before purchasing it as a domain name.

▶ Try to never start a domain name or email address with the letter "I" or "L". Both of these letters are very hard to distinguish from each other. If the lower case "L" is used, it is hard to distinguish it from the letter "I" or even the number "1" making it easier for a person to make a typo when typing in your website address or trying to send you an email.

▶ Choose a domain name that will appear closer to the top of directories where you will be submitting your URL for a listing. Most directories are listed in alphabetical order so try to choose a domain name that is not only easy to remember and type, but also one that starts with a letter of the alphabet (or a number) that will be as closest to the letter "A" as possible. For example: My old website at columbusnotary.com started with the letter "C." If I had chosen a domain name of ohionotary.com instead – the "O" would appear lower on the list than the "C" since the directories are listed in alphabetical order.

But don't get clever and seek a domain name like "AAAAA1111." Naturally this would appear at the top of directories but when you repeat a letter or number more than two times in a row – people have a hard time typing it. To see what I mean, try saying "AAAAA1111" out loud. Can you immediately recognize how many times the "A" is repeated? Not many other people will either and it will cause you major problems later on down the road. (Even the auto club AAA uses the terminology "triple A" so people will know how many "A's" there are in their company name).

Why Do I Need a Web Page for Marketing?

After you understand what domain names are and have selected one for yourself, you should go ahead and

purchase it before someone else registers it. Although I
suggest you use Bummer Hosting http://
www.bummerhosting.com) to register your domain
name, you may choose any other company you want to
do the job. The current prices for registering a domain
name for two years is under $30 so don't allow yourself
to be ripped-off.

Now, all that's left to do is make your web page and
upload it to the internet so we can begin learning how
to market your services all over the United States. But
many people are afraid of this step because they don't
understand how simple and easy it is to design a web
page. If you can use your word processing program,
you can make a web page just as quickly and easily.
One excellent place for beginners to go on the internet
to learn how to design a web page is at http://
www.pagetutor.com/. Or, get a copy of my book "*My
Homemade Business*". An entire section (including
computer screenshots) is dedicated to teaching you step
by step how to design a basic web page. Free software,
graphics and web page templates are included for
internet download. For more information, go to http://
www.50statenotary.com/marketingbook/

So far, you have accomplished a lot. But even if you
are the best NSA on the planet earth, you will not make
any money unless you learn how to market your services. The next section will help get you started on the
right path to marketing.

SECTION 3

Marketing Your Business

---

*For wisdom is a defence, and money is a defence:
but the excellency of knowledge is, that wisdom
giveth life to them that have it.*

Ecclesiastes 7:12

Developing a Mindset for Marketing

Even if you do have the determination, drive and ability to own and operate your own business right now, when you do decide to open a business – if you do not understand marketing and how to do it, your business will fail. I know this is true because I have developed many good products in the past but my marketing failed. I then took this same material, repackaged it and marketed it a little differently and made great money. So the problem was not in my product – it was the marketing technique I used to sell the product.

Marketing is very simple to describe. It is the method you use to sell a product or service. In fact, you are already experienced in marketing, but you may not realize it. When you applied for a job, you probably looked through the newspaper, made yourself a resume and sent your resume out hoping to get a call for an interview. Do you know you just did? You marketed yourself? How?

First, when you looked in the newspaper to find a job you looked for jobs that fit your skills. If you want to work as a secretary, you certainly would not send your resume to a trucking company who is seeking a warehouse dockworker. The act of looking for a job to fit your skills is the same concept as "target marketing." Target marketing simply means that you locate a market (group) of people who would be interested in what you are selling or the service you perform. For example, an experienced notary would seek their target market of customers in the real estate and legal industry since they utilize notaries the most.

Continuing with our example, the next thing you did when you found a job in the newspaper that you might be interested in applying for – you sent them your resume. As a business owner seeking to obtain customers for your business, you essentially do the same thing. But instead of a resume, you will send what is called a "cover letter" that is prepared on your company letterhead.

A typical cover letter sample appears on Page 81.

Notice the way the letter is setup. There should always be a "Re:" line on any business letter. "Re" stands for the word "regarding." The "regarding" is two or three words that provide the main subject matter of the letter. This way, the person receiving the letter can quickly glance through all their correspondence and pick out the letters they want to handle first. By including a "Re:" line, you are showing the company you respect their time and consideration, which indicates to them that you would be a notary that may be pleasant and easy to work with.

Do not confuse the "Re" line of a business letter with an opportunity to advertise. The purpose of the "Re" line is to be courteous to the receiver so they can quickly glance and prioritize your correspondence from the stack of mail they received that day. NEVER use the "Re" line to try and sell them something.

**QUICK
TIP**

Your Company Name
Address
City, State, Zip
Telephone Number, Fax Number
Email and URL

Date

Mr. John Doe
ABC Mortgage Company
123 Main Street
Anytown, VA 24283-0849

Re: Notary Public Services

Dear Mr. Doe:

I am an independent notary public who serves the Anytown county area. I am contacting you to introduce my services and to ask you to keep my company in mind if you should need notarial services for your clients in the near future.

I am available to your clients 24-hours a day and am very experienced in many areas of the mortgage document process. I have enclosed a list of mortgage, title and signing companies I have worked with in the past for your review.

If you feel my services would benefit your company, please contact me to arrange an appointment at a time convenient for you. I look forward in hearing from you soon.

Sincerely,

Your Name
Notary Public

Sample Cover Letter

Another Exercise in Understanding Marketing

Suppose you wanted to sell your old car in order to buy another one. What would be the first step you would take? Normally it would be to call the local newspaper and place an ad. But what would you say in your ad? Would you say something like: *"Green car I absolutely love is for sale."* Of course not!! You would say something like *"1986 Ford Escort, 102,000 miles, fair condition, $800."*

What did you just do? You provided precise information about the year and make of the car, the mileage, the condition and the price. In addition, you listed this car for sale under "Automobiles for Sale." You didn't list it in the obituaries. That's called proper marketing and you do things like this every day.

But don't make the mistake of trying to sell lots of different products and services at one time just because you desperately want to make money. Doing this makes it hard to concentrate on selling one specific product or service and you will never be a success. (I know this from personal experience). Make sure you have ONE major product or service line, and you can add other products and services that are associated with the main one. That way — you can market your products and services to a specific market and be able to market and sell in specific terms.

Let's go back to the sample classified ad for selling your automobile for a moment. What if your ad said "Green car I absolutely love is for sale plus I knit baby booties, trade stocks and bonds and do yard work for fun." Does this tell anybody anything? Absolutely not! It confuses people and they will pass your ad by. You will never sell your car this way — just like you will not sell your products and services by marketing in the same manner. In marketing, you need to find a specific target market and provide that specific market with products and services they are interested in buying.

Also Remember to Be Humble

Although I could write a 10,000-page book on marketing, the purpose of this section is to provide you with the basics so you can learn the rest on your own. And one the biggest mistakes people make running their own business is their lack of ability to be humble.

Have you ever watched success stories on television of people who really succeeded at their own businesses? The Food Network has an excellent program called "<u>Food Finds</u>" where they actually visit the shops of small family-owned businesses and interview the owners. Every successful business owner will say the same thing: *"We care about what our customer wants and we do everything to provide it."* I have NEVER heard a successful business owner say something like: *"I am a mean, hateful person who despises people and I don't allow any idiot to take advantage of me. If they don't want to pay my price that's fine – let them go some-where else."*

But very often I find new business owners taking this same selfish attitude with potential customers and

other business professionals. One way I can immediately spot a person like this is when I find a notary who
refuses to help another notary because they think they
will steal work away from them. I receive emails from
notaries who tell me how uncooperative other notaries
are when they try to contact them for help. Some
notaries are either "brushed off" and others have actually been treated rudely. As I have stated in previous
articles I have written for The Notary News – when you
find a notary with an attitude like this – walk away and
find a notary who doesn't have this attitude. The reason
any notary would have an attitude like this is because
they are selfish and inexperienced in business. So one
of the greatest lessons you need to learn is humility in
order to be a successful business owner. In other words
– you have to place the needs of your customers and
business contacts above your own.

I realize that adapting these traits may be difficult
for some people to do. The world today educates people
into believing that they are the only person that matters. The world will tell you that you deserve this and
that and you need to be pampered because they want
to sell you a new product. Don't believe me? Turn on
your television and tune it to a shopping network.
Spend at least 30 minutes listening to exactly how
products are presented. It doesn't matter what the
product is or whether you would buy it or not. What you
are looking for is how often the salesperson explains
how this wonderful product will benefit you and your life
because you are the only person that matters in the
world. Pampering the ego of a customer is just one
marketing technique but there are millions more.

In my opinion, the shopping networks have some of the best salespeople in the world. You never find them to be pushy or hateful (like some used car salespeople). Instead, they are caring, kind and considerate people who seem to show a genuine concern for making your life easier by selling you a product to do just that. When people who have purchased the product in the past call into the program, the salespeople are always very nice and cheerful. They pay compliments to the caller and use sales tactics to re-enforce to them that they made the perfect choice by purchasing this product. The caller naturally agrees this is the best product since sliced bread and this in turn boosts sales.

But what most people don't think about is that these salespeople are there to earn a salary and sell their client's products. PERIOD. Although they may be nice people in real life, they certainly have a different voice when interacting with customers and clients than they do when they interact off camera. And their interaction with customers is always humble, courteous and helpful. These salespeople are being humble and considerate so they can sell more products.

You will have to adapt the same type of humbleness toward anyone you come into contact with in your business (regardless if they are customers or not) to be successful in your business. If you cannot do that at the present time, I would suggest you get on your knees and go to God in prayer, asking Him to heal your mind. Or you could take a "anger management" class and learn how to deal with your negative emotions because they will prevent you from growing your business.

An Email Communication Tip

A majority of your marketing will be done by email. As you communicate with people, they will learn to trust you as well as your products and services. However, some people do not properly communicate in their emails so here is an important tip to help you avoid the major problem in email communications.

If I sent you an email that said: "The Big Bear is being replaced by Giant Eagle." you probably would have no idea what I was talking about. First you would try to figure out what "Big Bear" and "Giant Eagle" meant. You would surmise that these must be important names because they are capitalized – but you still don't have enough information to go on.

At this point you have only three possible choices:

▶ Delete the email and forget about it;
▶ Reply to my email and ask me to what I am referring to; or
▶ Take a guess.

Most people do not like to appear that they misunderstood something, so the majority of people faced with this or a similar situation will try to guess at the meaning. If you live in California, you may think "Big Bear" is referring to Big Bear Lake. If you live in Arizona on an Indian Reservation, you may think "Big Bear" is an Indian name and refers to an actual person. And if by some chance another person with an Indian name of "Giant Eagle" existed – my email could be totally misunderstood and cause my Indian friend to tell others about how a man named Big Bear is near death and will be replaced by a man named Giant Eagle. (Sound too far-fetched? Misunderstandings that turn into catastrophes like this happen every single day).

But if you lived in Columbus, Ohio – you would automatically understand that "Big Bear" and "Giant Eagle" are two grocery store chains. So in my original email I should have really said: "The Big Bear grocery store is being replaced by the Giant Eagle grocery store." By simply adding the words "grocery store" for clarity – I could send my email to anyone in the world and they would probably understand what it meant without question.

The point is that YOU need to think about the person receiving your email before you click the SEND button. Just because you understand what your email means, doesn't mean the person receiving your email will know what you mean. I get emails from people (including attorneys) every week with messages like: *"I contacted you about 9 months ago. Do you remember me?"* There is no name, no phone number and no other information but I am supposed to remember some unknown person that emailed me 9 months ago. Come on folks! I don't know of anyone on the planet earth who could do this.

Or perhaps you are one of those people like me. You always make sure you write clear and concise emails. You also review them before clicking the SEND button and you consider yourself to be pretty good with your email communication. But one day you get an email like "The Big Bear is being replaced by Giant Eagle." Which one of the three choices previously listed would you choose to do in order to handle this email? Would you choose to "guess" at the meaning like everyone else? If so, you need to think about a very simple solution – and that is to simply click the "REPLY" button and say: *"Please clarify your statements so that I may sufficiently handle your request."*

Fraudulent Marketing Techniques

Finally, you need to be alerted about not developing fraudulent techniques in the marketing of your own products and services. Just like when people lie and fraudulently misrepresent themselves on a resume (we all have done this at one point in our careers) do not carry this trait into the advertising and marketing of your business. You will always find that any dollar you steal from one person will cost you hundreds of dollars in the near future.

Let me give you an example of what I am talking about. Back is the early 1980's a guy ran a mail order business ad that said: *"How to Not Pay Any Land Taxes. Send $5 to PO Box X.."* It was rumored that this man received over 100,000 inquiries. What did this guy do to fill the customer's order and not be accused of mail fraud? Everyone who sent him $5 was sent a piece of paper with the words: *"Live on a boat."*

Since this man did not commit mail fraud; since this man provided a service by fulfilling the answer to the question in his ad; and since the man provided a legally sound answer – he committed no crime and he made half a million dollars. (Note: If you live on a boat, there are no land taxes because a boat does not sit on land).

However, this type of marketing is still fraudulent. How do you think the person who sent in the $5 felt when they received the message back in the mail that they had to live on a boat in order to avoid paying land taxes? They probably felt stupid and ripped-off at the same time. Do you think they will ever do business with this guy again? Of course not.

Remember this lesson in your day-to-day life working in the real estate industry. If you get a bad reputation in this industry, word will get around fast. Be honest and truthful in all your dealings and word of your dependability and quality of work will get around the real estate world very quickly also. This type of success and reputation cannot be bought at any price. It is genuine and it will certainly enable you as a business owner to become very successful and financially secure compared to using fraudulent techniques that put you out of business fast.

Internet Marketing Tips for NSA's

Once you have secured a domain name and have a website established on the internet, you can start marketing your services online. The first step is to make sure you have the proper META tags on all your web pages. META "keywords" tags are words that people would type in a search engine if they were seeking your services. For instance, a NSA website should contain at the minimum the following META "keywords" tags on every one of their web pages:

▶ notary
▶ notary public
▶ notary signing agent
▶ notarization

If you do not know what META tags are and how to insert them into your web pages, an excellent tutorial is located online at http://www.freewebmastertips.com/ (Click on META Tutorials). Another fantastic website for educating yourself on HTML and Javascript is located at http://www.htmlgoodies.com/.

The main thing that confuses people about META tags is that they appear in HTML code. The software you used to design your web pages should have some way to insert META tags, but if it doesn't — you will need to go into the Windows Notepad (Start > Programs > Accessories > Notepad) on your computer, open up your web page in Notepad and insert your META tags manually.

META tags start with the HTML code <head> and end with </head>. The slash "/" is inserted before the command "head" to turn the feature off. In between the <head> and </head> will be other HTML commands, but the one that you are most concerned with is the META tag named "keywords." When you open up your web page in the Windows Notepad, the keywords tag looks like this:

<META NAME="keywords" CONTENT="notary, notary public, notary signing agent, notarization">

If your web page does not contain this line in the
META tag area, type it in manually. It should be placed
under the META tag named "title" which indicates the
title name of your web page. You may use up to 800
characters in the keywords area. Just make sure you
place the most important keywords at the beginning,
making sure you do not repeat them over and over
again. Some search engines ignore websites with multiple uses of the same keyword and will label them as
spam.

Listing with Search Engines

As you submit your web site to search engines
(which is accomplished by filling out a form), a tool
called a "spider" will go to your website, read your META
tags and categorize your web site. Then, when someone
goes to the search engine and types in the word "notary" or "notary public" your web site will be displayed.

Some places to submit your website to search engines are:

- ▶ http://www.google.com/addurl.html
- ▶ http://www.submitexpress.com/
- ▶ http://submitit.bcentral.com/msnsubmit.htm
- ▶ http://addurl.alltheweb.com/add_url

To find more, go to any search engine and type in
the search words "submit URL" and start going through
the links. You will find many places that offer you a
choice of a free listing or paid listing. If you decide to
pay for a listing, make sure you read and understand

the benefits. Often, you may be able to manually submit your website to each search engine yourself (but there are thousands of them). Although this process will take more time, it will give you some good internet experience plus save you a ton of money in your advertising budget.

QUICK TIP

Before submitting your website to search engines sign up and get a free email account at Yahoo, Hotmail, etc. As you fill out the forms to submit your URL, use this email address instead. All search engines you submit your website to will send you a confirmation, plus they may sell your email address and you will be bombarded with a lot of junk mail. Keep a separate email account for your marketing so can prevent spam coming to your private email account.

After you submit your website to search engines you may want to know how to get your web site at the top of the list. There is really no great science to this. While there are lots of power marketing gurus who are anxious to sell you books on how to get listed at the top of search engines, I have accomplished the same task without spending any money.

What worked for me was going to a search engine (I prefer Google at http://www.google.com). I typed in the words "notary signing agent" and visited the websites of the first 4 or 5 websites that appeared in the search. Then I viewed the "keywords" they used in listing their web page.

QUICK TIP

To view keywords used on a webpage from Internet Explorer, allow the web page to completely load. Click on "View" then select the "Source" option. Not all web pages will allow you to view their source information, but the majority of them do.

Next, I revised the keywords in my META tags (if appropriate) and resubmitted my website to the Google search engine.

Another way to get your web pages listed at the top of search engines is by generating a lot of traffic (visitors to your web site). The more visitors your website receives, the more your web page will move up on the search engine list. While this is not true for every search engine, it has worked for me in the past.

I do not consider myself to be a great power marketing internet guru — so I urge you to check out some of these websites for more information:

▶   http://www.internetmarketingconference.com/
▶   http://www.dotfactor.com/

▶ http://www.onlinewebtraining.com/
▶ http://www.searchengineworkshops.com/
▶ http://insite.lycos.com/tutorial.asp

Or, go to any search engine and type in the words:
"internet power marketing," or "marketing on the internet," or "search engine marketing" or even "internet marketing tutorials" to find more links.

FOR AOL USERS

If you access the internet through AOL (America Online) you may not be able to access some areas of the internet. This is because AOL places blocks on certain keywords to protect their users from spam. If you wish to view the entire internet without any restrictions, do the following:

▶ Log on to the internet through AOL as you normally do.

▶ Minimize the AOL browser.

▶ Click on Internet Explorer (the lower case letter "E" on your desktop) and use Internet Explorer to surf the internet.

Other Ways for NSAs to Make Money

The heart of him that hath understanding seeketh knowledge: but the mouth of fools feedeth on foolishness.

Proverbs 15:14

Other Ways for NSA's to Increase Their Income

As an NSA, you do not have to limit yourself to loan document signings. There are a number of ways you can still make money as a notary and provide a great service to the public. But before I provide you with these suggestions I want to address a very important issue that confuses a lot of people, which is: You can have multiple business names without obtaining an EIN (Employer Identification Number) or business license. The only time you would need to obtain these licenses would be if you decide to hire employees. And even if you do reach a point where you need to hire employees – you can hire independent people like yourself and pay them an hourly salary. You only need to have them sign a Contractor's Agreement basically stating that they will be responsible for the reporting of their own taxes. And if you pay a contract employee more than $600 in a 12 month period, you will need to file a Form 1099 with the government (which is why the W9 form is used by companies you sign up with to do closings for). This process is much easier than obtaining an EIN number, a business license, separate business bank account, paying social security taxes on the wages you pay an employee, etc.

With this in mind – you can have 100 different business names and you will not violate any legal regulations by not applying for an EIN number or business license for each one unless you decide to hire employees. You can have a company named "Jerry's Notary Services" and another business named "Jerry's Title Company" and another business named "Jerry's

Chocolate Chip Cookies." The combined money all your businesses earn is reported on Form 1040 of your personal income taxes at the end of the year, and out of that income you are allowed a wide range of exemptions for operating the businesses. None of this requires an EIN number or a business license issued by your state.

With that knowledge in mind, I will provide you with some excellent ideas for adding on to your existing NSA business, or for opening a separate business under a different name.

Home Inspections

One company named MortgageRamp provides additional income for notaries who are interested in doing home inspections. Some of the home inspections are simple drive-bys where you take a few pictures with your digital camera and email them back to MortgageRamp with your report. Visit their website at http://www.mortgageramp.com/ and check out this opportunity if you think you would enjoy this type of work. There are companies other than MortgageRamp who employ notaries for this same service, but I have personal experience with MortgageRamp and know them to be a reputable company to work with).

Hospitals

Most hospitals have a notary working onsite but the notary is normally available only during business hours. You can either write a professional letter to the Hospital Administrator or visit the office of the Administrator informing them that you are available after hours and weekends. This schedule works well for notaries who are employed full-time outside their home because they can do mobile signings after working hours. This technique has worked well for me. Normally I am called to hospitals to notarize Power of Attorney documents so that a family member may conduct some business on behalf of the person in the hospital. I have also notarized Last Wills and Testaments for patients who only have days or hours left to live.

On Page 100 is a sample letter to send to Hospital Administrators.

Elderly and Disabled People

Elderly and disabled people can bring you lots of repeat business. They often need Power of Attorney's, stock certificates, trusts and other documents notarized. Because you will travel to the elderly person's home at a time convenient for them, they are normally grateful for this benefit and will recommend you to others. Advertise your services in your local yellow pages under "Notary Public" or mail an introductory letter and business card to area nursing homes and senior centers.

Convalescent Homes

With the permission of the Administrator, you can post flyers or pass out business cards to patients and staff in convalescent homes. While these people do not need loan signings, they often need Powers of Attorney, grant deeds, wills and other documents notarized.

Your Company Name
Address
City, State, Zip
Telephone Number, Fax Number
Email and URL

Name of Hospital Administrator
Title of Hospital Administrator
Name of Hospital
Address
City, State and Zip

Re: Notary Public Services

Dear Mr. or Mrs. Whoever:

What would happen if a patient or a member of your staff needed a notary public immediately and your onsite notary was not available? This can be a crucial situation if a patient is terminally ill and needs a Will, power of attorney or other legal document notarized during hours when your onsite notary is unavailable. Because of these reasons, I would like to make you aware that I am a mobile notary public, available during all hours for emergency notary public services and I am located in the same area of your hospital.

Please alert your hospital staff, as well as your onsite notary public of my services and feel free to contact me at any time that I may be of service to you, your staff or the patients in your hospital. I have enclosed a business card to keep in a convenient area for your future use.

Thank you for your time and consideration.

Sincerely,

Your Name
Notary Public

Sample Letter to Hospitals

These people are normally unable to leave the convalescent home and if they can travel, the whole experience is normally traumatic for them. You eliminate these problems by offering mobile notary services, which will bring you lots of repeat business.

Notarizing Depositions

Market your notary services to smaller law firms (and court reporters) that employ notaries for notarizing depositions. Many different types of law firms, especially law firms relating to personal injury and litigation, do depositions.

A deposition is done in the presence of a court reporter, the person answering the questions in the deposition, the attorney for the plaintiff and the attorney for the defendant. The services of a notary are required to notarize the deposition stating the statements made by the party in the deposition are accurate. Because notarizations must be done by a notary who has no personal interest or gain in the legal matter, attorneys often employ independent notaries to sit in at depositions and some of them pay as much as $200 a day.

Working for a Probate Attorney

Probate attorneys draft wills, power of attorneys and other documents to facilitate probate proceedings upon the death of a person. The attorney cannot prepare the documents and notarize them also because it would be a conflict of interest. If the probate attorney is working independently he or she would be a good candidate to contact as someone who may need your services. You would work on an "as needed" basis and be paid a certain fee for each document you notarized.

Of course the fee you are paid by the attorney would be more than $1 or $2 because travel expenses need to be factored into your fee. If the attorney decides to use your services on a continual basis, you could set up an account for the attorney and bill him or her on a monthly basis. Attorneys like this and they don't have to pay you in "dibs and drabs."

Work for/with Another Notary

If you lack the experience, one idea would be to network with experienced notaries in your area. If the experienced notary is now working for signing companies exclusively, you can share the knowledge you learned in this book and help them market their services to mortgage and title companies. As you know, mortgage and title companies only employ experienced notaries (unless you know someone personally who manages or owns a mortgage or title company and is willing to give you a chance), so your experienced notary friend should be the one marketing to these types of companies to help bring both of you more work.

You then would work for your experienced notary friend when a signing assignment was issued by the mortgage or title company. Because the mortgage or title company pays more money (some pay as high as $300 per signing) you and your notary friend can split the money or set up a payment structure so the notary completing the assignment receives 75% and the other receives a 25% referral fee. You will make more money in the long run because the mortgage and title company will normally provide you with more work (depending on your area of course). So even if the mortgage or title company pays you and your friend $150 (instead of $300) you will make it up in volume and actually earn more money compared to working for a signing company. Plus, you build up a steady stream of work if your clients are mortgage and title companies versus signing companies.

Market Yourself to Real Estate Agents

There are probably hundreds of real estate agents in your area and these people are in touch with the entire mortgage loan process. I know several notaries who work for real estate agents. They schedule a time with the agent, arrive at their office and notarize the documents. One notary told me the real estate agent she works with actually set her up an office space so she could do notarizations with clients in a more private atmosphere. Another real estate agent has so much business they schedule several notarizations at the same time. The notary arrives at the scheduled time and completes all the signings at once – rather than having to drive back and forth for each one.

Advertise in the Yellow Pages

If you live in a major city, advertising in the local Yellow Pages may be expensive. In addition, the Yellow

Pages are only published once a year. However, if you can get listed as a Notary Public in your local Yellow Pages you will find that it brings you a lot of business. Check your local phone company for rates and deadline dates.

Set Up a Title Company

Setting up a title company is easy. Select a name for your business and you are ready to go to work. A title search is done for all real estate transactions to ensure that the seller of the property has the right to sell the property to the purchaser or to use the property as the security for a loan. Here is basically how the process works:

▶ The real estate attorney, mortgage company or title company hiring you to conduct a title search for them will initially provide you with the following types of information:

▷ Legal description of the property. A sample of what a property's legal description looks like is:

> BEGIN at an iron pin at the intersection of the western right-of-way at Beaver Road (50-foot right-of-way) and the northeastern right-of-way at the Chesapeake Railroad; thence, run north 58 degrees, 12 minutes, 18 seconds west 57.57 feet to an iron pin placed; thence, run in a northwesterly direction along the arc of a curve and arc distance of 587.23 feet, to an iron pin (said curve having a radius of

583.44 feet, and being subtended by a chord bearing north 28 degrees, 18 minutes, 21 seconds west) ….. etc.

QUICK TIP

If the title search is being prepared in connection with a sale, the Sale's Contract will have the legal description of the property. If the title search is being done in connection with a mortgage loan, the loan application usually contains a legal description of the property.

▷ The name of the current owner of the property.

▷ Copies of all deeds, surveys or any prior title examination or title insurance policies that affect the property.

These three pieces of information are the minimum the company should provide to you. Some companies hiring you to do a title search will be more established and provide you with much more information to make your job easier.

▶ After you receive this information you will begin the process of the title search on the property. If you have ever done family tree research or worked for an attorney that required you to do research – you will love working as a title searcher. These skills are needed to do a good job.

How to Do a Title Search

Title searches are usually done at the courthouse of the county where the property is located. If the property is located in two or more counties (which rarely occurs) you will have to do a title search in two or more counties and provide two or more reports of your findings. The public official who is responsible for keeping real property records varies from state to state, but this person is normally called the Clerk of Courts or Registrar of Deeds. The real property records are kept in a record room located within the county courthouse.

Many larger cities now make it possible to do title searches online from the comfort of your home. To find out if your local court has an online website, do the following:

▶ Go to http://www.findlaw.com/11stategov/

▶ Scroll down to your state and click on its link

▶ At the next page, scroll down to the "Courts" link and select it

▶ From here you can find the links to the courts in your state.

To search court records, you need a USERID and password issued by PACER. On Page 116, under the subtitle of "Bankruptcy Foreclosures" I will provide you with step-by-step instructions for establishing your own free PACER account.

Full-Length and Limited Title Searches

Now that you know where to go to find information for your title search, you now need to determine what period of time you need to cover in your title search. If you are doing a full-length title search you will need to go back in the records 50 or 60 years (or when the house was first built). From there you create a "owner's chain" which is similar to charting a family tree in a genealogy research. You start with the first owner's name and trace the ownership of the house through to the present owner.

However, most title searches you will be doing will be "limited" searches. If this loan is for a second mortgage, the full-length title search has already been done when the first mortgage was obtained. Therefore, you only need to do a title search beginning from the recording date of the first mortgage. Or, if the property owner has a copy of a previous full-title examination, you may also only need to do a limited search. I am sure the company that hires you to do the title search will inform you what length of search they need so you can price your services accordingly.

Grantee and Grantor Indexes

So now that you know what point in time to begin your title search, you need to know where to start looking for the information to complete your examination. Using the search capabilities on the website of your local county court or by visiting the courthouse in person, you would ask the Clerk of Courts where the

Grantee and Grantor Index is located and begin your search.

A **"<u>Grantee</u>"** index is an alphabetical index by last name of all people who PURCHASED property during a specific year within that particular county. Grantee's can also be holders of mortgages and security deeds, easement holders, tenants, holders of liens and so on.

A **"<u>Grantor</u>"** index is an alphabetical index by last name of all people who SOLD property during a specific year within that particular county. Grantor's can be sellers, borrower(s), mortgagors, grantors of easements and so on.

These indexes are maintained on a yearly basis beginning at a point in time when the county court began keeping records. Remember that every courthouse will have a different way of doing things – so you may have to do several title searches before you "learn the ropes" at your particular courthouse.

You will begin with the GRANTOR index from the past and follow it to the present. You then start with the last GRANTEE that was found in the Grantee Index and compare it to the Grantor Index until this person's name (you are seeking) is found and there is a transfer of the property from them. Like I said, this is the same thing as family tree research. If you think of the process in this simplistic manner, it will ease any intimidation you may feel about doing title searches.

Copies of your findings should be made to provide to the client hiring you to do the title search. Just like with family tree research, you need to document and provide proof to back up your title search report.

Plat Index

Most counties maintain a plat or tract index and copies of all the plats that have been recorded within the county. Once you have located the plat for the property you are doing the title search for, you will locate a property description. This property description should match the property description provided to you by whoever employed you to do the title search. Any discrepancies should be noted.

Plats often have restrictive covenants printed on them that are binding on an owner of the property. Plats also show building setback lines, easements and other matters. Most courthouses have photocopy equipment to enable you to make a copy of the plat and it is suggested that you request a copy be made for the attorney (if applicable) as well as the client you are working for.

Reviewing Deeds, Easements or Mortgages

From the information on the plat you can easily find the deeds, easements or mortgages associated with a particular piece of property. All of these documents will contain a copy of the legal description. You may find the legal description changes over the course of time. This is not unusual and it may be due to a current parcel of property that may have been included within larger tracts in past history. The information you will provide to your client should be the following:

▶ Note the identity of the parties listed on the document, the date the document was signed and the date it was filed with the courthouse. (Court documents are file and date stamped by the court).

▶ Note the signature and witnessing requirements.

▶ Make a notation of how the real estate was conveyed to the next party (for example: fee simple, life estate, etc.)

▶ List any covenants or other requirements that may be noted in the documents.

Searching for Liens

After you have traced the "ownership chain" of the property from the point of time required by your client to the present owner, you now need to search for liens on the property. There are several different types of liens that are extremely important for you to know about when dealing with real property. These include:

▶ Judgment liens;
▶ Federal and State tax liens;
▶ Delinquent taxes;
▶ Uniform Commercial Code;
▶ Lis pendens;
▶ Civil suits;
▶ Probate court proceedings;
▶ Mechanic's liens; and
▶ Bankruptcy foreclosures.

Judgment Liens

A money debt resulting from a lawsuit is called a judgment. Once a judgment is recorded in the public records it becomes a lien on all property of the person who was sued and lost in the lawsuit. A docket or index for judgments can be found in the real property record room. The docket list is in alphabetical order and contains the names of all people within the county within a given year who had a judgment lien recorded. The index also refers to a book and page of a judgment book in which a copy of the judgment can be found.

The index does not contain the amount of the judgment or whether the judgment has been paid or satisfied. Therefore, you will need to obtain a copy of the judgment in the judgment book to find out. Most clerks print the word "Paid" or "Satisfied" on a judgment when it has been paid. Judgments in most states have only a 7-year lifespan, but they may be renewed for an additional 7 years. Because judgment liens attach themselves to all property of the person who was sued and lost in the lawsuit, it is necessary for you to examine the judgment index for the names of ALL people who have owned the property during the lifetime of a judgment (7 years unless renewed).

Federal and State Tax Liens

The federal and state government has the right to file a lien against the property of any taxpayer that is delinquent on their income taxes. Once a tax lien is filed, the lien applies to all property owned by the taxpayer at the time of filing as well as all future property the taxpayer obtains until the debt is paid.

Most record rooms maintain a separate index for federal tax liens and a separate book in which the federal tax liens can be looked at. A federal tax lien has a 10-year lifespan unless renewed. A state tax lien has its own statute of limitations and varies from state to state.

At the time of this writing, there is pending legislation to change the 10-year lifespan of a federal and state tax lien to non-expiring and the renewal would be eliminated. Be sure and check the current legislation when you encounter a federal or state tax lien on a piece of real estate that is more than 10 years old.

Delinquent Taxes

All real property is taxed by the county or city government and may be separately taxed for sanitary, sewer or other services. These tax liabilities and other assessments become liens on the property. Liens for assessments may be found in a tax assessor's or tax collector's office, which may be separate and apart from the real property record room.

In many cities and towns there are specialized tax services that examine tax and assessment records for a reasonable price and most title searchers and law firms use these services to find out the tax obligations of a particular piece of property.

Uniform Commercial Code

When personal property is involved it will be necessary for you to search the Uniform Commercial Code financing statement index to find out if any of the personal property has been pledged as security for a loan. (Real property is any structure attached to "God's Green Earth" [actual legal description] and personal property is anything else, such as motor vehicles, clothing, antiques, etc.) For example, suppose someone was purchasing a piece of property and they placed a lien on their $25,000 mink coat to secure the loan. The mink coat is personal property. It is not attached to "God's Green Earth" and it is not a structure.

The index of the Uniform Commercial Code is an alphabetical listing by last name of all persons who have pledged personal property as security for a loan. In states that also have central filing of UCC financing statements with the Secretary of State's office, a state search must be conducted as well as a local search.

Lis Pendens

I bet most of you never heard of the words "Lis Pendens" until now. Well listen up and impress your business associates by using the term correctly. A lawsuit that affects the title to real estate that has not been paid or resolved, and is still pending, does NOT affect title to the property unless a LIS PENDENS is filed on the real property records. A lis pendens (pronounced "liz pen dens") charges third parties with notice that an action is pending against a certain piece of property and that if they purchase the property or obtain a loan on the property, they will be bound by the previous judgment in the lawsuit. A lis pendens does NOT apply to judgments obtained on a lawsuit for a personal or money judgment. Lis pendens are only applicable when the lawsuit action directly affects title to the property.

A lis pendens is normally a simple document that gives notice that a lawsuit has been filed as well as information about the lawsuit. This information is:

▶ Name of the court in which the lawsuit was filed;
▶ The parties involved;
▶ A civil action file number; and
▶ A brief description of the nature of the lawsuit.

Most counties maintain separate records for lis pendens. The record index is maintained alphabetically by the last name of the property owner.

Civil Suits

Normally a pending civil suit (regardless of the nature) has little or no effect on title to real property unless a lis pendens notice has been recorded. But to do your job thoroughly as a title searcher you need to examine the civil dockets for information purposes. For example, if a borrower(s) is in the process of purchasing property from a seller and you find a number of lawsuits on the civil docket against the seller for breach of contract, the borrower(s) (as well as whoever hired you to conduct the title search) should be advised to be cautious and aware.

Probate Court Proceedings

Due to the death of property owners, a piece of property may pass through probate court. As a title searcher you will need to examine the probate court records to make sure the Will is properly probated and the property has been distributed to the heirs in the case of an interstate (within the same state) estate. Also, if the executor of an estate has sold the property, you need to search the probate or estate records to find out if the proper authority for the sale of the property have been obtained by the executor.

Mechanic's Liens

A mechanics' lien or assessment given to a contractor, laborer, or material supplier who has done construction on the property may be found in the Grantor Index or in a separate index. It may be easier for you to remember what a Mechanic's Lien is by associating the word "mechanic" with a person who works on your car. When your car needs fixed you take it to a mechanic. When a house needs repairs and improvements, the owners hire contractors, laborers or other material suppliers to fix or improve the property. If the owners do not pay these people for the repairs, a Mechanic's Lien will be filed at the courthouse.

Bankruptcy Foreclosures

In some cases you may be doing a title search on a property that may be in the process of foreclosure and a bankruptcy has been filed by the owner of the property.

About 75% of the bankruptcy courts in all 50 states are currently available online for record searching. The only thing you need to search these files is a PACER login and ID. PACER stands for **P**ublic **A**ccess to **C**ourt **E**lectronic **R**ecords. There is no cost to obtain a PACER login and ID. Just go online to http://www.pacer.psc.uscourts.gov/register.html, fill out the form and one will be mailed to you.

Once you have been mailed your PACER login and ID, do the following:

▶ Login to http://www.pacer.psc.uscourts.gov/

▶ Click on "Links to PACER Web Sites"

▶ Choose to search "Appeals," "Bankruptcy" or "District" courts

▶ Choose the court you want to search from the list

▶ Type in your PACER login and password to access the court

At the present time you are charged 7¢ per page you access and print out. Make sure you learn how to use PACER correctly so you don't waste money. PACER will send you a bill every three months. Make sure you pay the bill promptly or you could lose your account.

PACER provides excellent information on how to properly look up records in the court system to help you. Just go to http://www.pacer.psc.uscourts.gov/faq.html

and study this information so you will properly know how to use the system. Since this is something you will use daily as a title searcher, you need to know how to properly use PACER.

Build on Your Knowledge as a Title Searcher

After reading through the information about how to conduct a proper title search, you may be thinking, *"This sounds like it would take days and weeks to complete one title search and I don't understand legal language."* I realize the process may initially sound complicated – but once you do a couple title searches you will know more about where to go for the information at the courthouse and what information you need to obtain so the process will be faster. Most of the title searches you do will not require you to search all the records I have provided information for. For instance, if you are doing a title search for a piece of property and you encounter no judgment liens, you would not need to search for judgment liens since there are none.

Also, you do NOT need to know anything about legal terminology to conduct a title search because you are searching most records by a person's last name. Also, all of the information you are researching is public information. Anyone off the street can walk into the courthouse and search through public information.

For instance, here in Columbus Ohio, if you walk in the front door of the bankruptcy court and enter the Clerk of Courts office, the bankruptcy petitions that have been recently filed are laying on a table. You can go through the petitions and examine them to your hearts content without getting permission from anyone. This is your right as an American citizen so don't be afraid that someone at the courthouse is going to tell you that you cannot view certain records that are public information. In fact, you will find that most people working in the court system are eager to help you if you treat them with courtesy and respect and don't expect them to do your job for you.

To learn more about starting or expanding your business to offer title search services, there are several references on the web to help you out. Here are a couple I found to help you get started:

Title Search Training Course
http://www.learnanytime.net/titleab/

This course will take you from the beginning to the end of a full title exam. Take an address to the local county courthouse and follow the steps provided in this course. The website states: *"When you complete this course, you will have the knowledge to work for an attorney or title company as a Real Estate Title Abstractor. Working in the courthouse alongside attorneys and paralegals is a fun and exciting career. Whether part-time or full-time, the earning potential is unlimited!"*

Company That Provides Title Search Services
http://www.nationalabstract.com/

It would help you to view other websites of companies who provide title search services so you will know how to effectively price and market your own title search business. Aside from the prestigious company website mentioned above, you can also go to any search engine like Google (http://www.google.com) and type in the search words: "title research services." Go through several of these links and you will get a better idea about how these companies work so you can structure your own company better.

How to Start a Signing Company

As NSA's we are all familiar with signing companies. These are the companies we sign up with and do signings for. Signing companies are similar to "temporary agencies." The signing company receives an assignment from a mortgage or title company and they are responsible for having the documents signed, notarized and returned back to the mortgage or title company. The signing company will hire an independent notary (such as you or me) to properly notarize the documents and they pay us, just like a temporary agency would do only no taxes are deducted from our checks.

The reason some signing companies only pay you $50 to do a signing and others pay you $100 is because some signing companies charge the mortgage or title company less money in order to get the job. For instance, a mortgage company is seeking a signing company to complete the loan process. They call one signing company who quotes them a price of $200. Another quotes them $100. If the signing company who quoted a price of $100 to the mortgage/title company gets the job, then hires you to do the signing – it is impossible for them to pay you more than $50 or $75 maximum.

Signing companies need to make some profit per signing, so they will pay you the least they can for the
largest profit.

However, larger signing companies who either have
established contracts with mortgage and title companies
to use their services exclusively, or signing companies
who have previously established a reputation of good
service to the mortgage or title company – may be in a
position to demand more money to complete the loan
process and pay their NSA's a larger fee.

To start your own signing company, you will need to
market your company to mortgage and title companies
in order to obtain assignments directly from them. In
the beginning of your business, you should network with
two or three experienced NSA's in your area to provide
you with backup in case a mortgage company gives you
10 or 20 closings to do in one day (this is a possibility
so prepare yourself for this). As you work with the
mortgage or title company, and they are satisfied with
the quality of your work – they will refer more signing
assignments to you. At that point you will need to seek
additional notaries in the area to call for loan closing
assignments. This is where directories of notaries come
in handy. One large directory is 123 Notary at http://
www.123notary.com. Another directory is located on my
website at http://www.50statenotary.com/directory/ but
there are many more.

Please understand that directories of notaries are
not necessarily employers of notaries. You would not
believe how many people fax me their resume, W9

form, E&O Insurance and copy of their notary certificates hoping to register with my company. But the fact is – I do NOT employ notaries. I only run a directory where the notaries are listed. I then market this directory to companies who employ notaries inviting them to use the notaries listed in the directory for their next assignment. So make sure you know the company you are dealing with and what services they provide before faxing or emailing your information. When I receive resumes and W9 forms it indicates to me that the notary is a beginner and does not have any experience. Nowhere on my website do I ask for submissions of resumes – yet some people feel they will send them to me anyway without any regard to the fact that I just have to toss them in the trashcan and waste my fax paper and toner.

Signing companies must also be responsible for the following:

▶ Receiving the mortgage documents, making sure the entire package is complete with all the required documents and securing a notary.

▶ Mailing the documents by overnight mail (UPS or Fed-X) to the notary along with copies for the borrower(s).

▶ Providing a return overnight envelope for the notary to return the documents after the notarization.

▶ Receiving the documents after the signing has taken place and reviewing them to make sure they are notarized and properly signed.

▶ Ensuring the documents are returned to the mortgage or title company on a specific date so the loan can close.

▶ Maintaining a database of their notaries, tracking the assignments the notary completed, and finally paying the notary.

As you can see, since a signing company also has a lot of work to do before, during and after the notary receives a signing assignment, if they are only paid $100 by the mortgage or title company, they cannot pay the notary more than $40 or $50. Now you can under-stand "why" you are paid such low wages when you work with some signing companies. You just need to decide if you want to work for those wages or not.

Also, you should now also begin to understand some of the reasons why notaries are not paid on time or not paid at all. Some fraudulent operators will open a signing company, market their services to mortgage and title companies (usually by providing them with a really cheap rate per signing), send out the notaries, and when the mortgage/title company pays them – they close up the business, don't pay their notaries and keep all the money. Because of this reason, I personally feel a national company should establish a registration process where signing companies must meet a set of criteria before being "certified". Then, notaries would only work for "certified" companies. Perhaps you can form a group of notaries that feel the same way and push for this certification of signing companies in the future.

Additionally, some signing companies will skip one of the steps I provided above and instead of the notary sending the documents back to them for review, the notary will mail the documents back to the mortgage or title company directly. Signing companies that do this are often "lazy" and you may want to be cautious. That's because there are a lot of notaries that do not know how to do a proper loan signing. They make mistakes, miss pages that needed notarized, etc. If all notaries return the documents directly back to the mortgage/title company for the closing and there is a mistake – the mortgage company may not do business with the signing company again. Therefore, most good signing companies will have the notary return or fax the documents to them for review before sending them to their client (the mortgage/title company).

But this is not true in all cases. I worked for a signing company in Lancaster, Ohio and completed several assignments for them. They knew the quality of my work and they also knew that I didn't make mistakes on the documents I returned to them. After building up my good name and reputation with the signing company, they had me mail my documents directly to the mortgage/title company after the assignment was completed. This step made it easier for the signing company to do their job and they in turn paid me more money per signing.

Some signing companies are now requiring new notaries who sign up with them to take a test before they send them out on any assignments. This test should not be confused with the certification test administered by the National Notary Association. Instead, this is a test created by the signing company itself and was initially implemented because notaries in the past have made so many errors working for their company. Some of these notaries could have done such sloppy work that they caused the signing company to lose any future work from a mortgage/title company, so the signing company has to do something to keep this from happening again.

What would you do if you were a signing company and Mortgage Company A was sending you 10 orders every day. Then a couple of notaries (who could care less if they did a good job or not) messed up so bad that they caused you to lose any future business from Mortgage Company A. You probably would implement some sort of testing system also. So the next time you encounter a situation like this and you get angry and con- fused about it, put yourself in the other person's shoes for a moment. Perhaps if you understand what really goes on "behind the scenes" you will be more compliant with sign- ing companies who operate in this manner.

The Future for Signing Companies

Due to the excessive errors caused by a large major- ity of notaries, coupled with the fact that signing com- panies come and go very rapidly – some mortgage and title companies are seeking to employ independent notaries directly and eliminate the signing company (middle person). Based on this fact, I personally be- lieve that small signing companies will eventually be put out of business and only the "best of the bunch" will survive, but this is only my opinion.

As a real world comparison – suppose a secretary was getting ready to take a vacation and the employer needed a temporary to fill in for the secretary during his or her absence. The employer (compare to a mortgage/ title company) can either call a temporary service (compare to a signing company), employ an independent contractor (compare to a notary public), have another employee absorb the workload (compare to an in-house notary who is an actual employee of the mortgage/ title company), or do nothing and let the work pile up.

But how does a NSA or signing company get in touch with mortgage and title companies in the first place to obtain work? This topic will be covered next.

How to Work Directly for Mortgage and Title Companies and Earn More Money

At first you may wonder why a mortgage or title company would employ an independent notary to directly work for them. Some people think title companies work only for the mortgage company and vise versa. But this is not entirely true. While it is true that title companies work directly for mortgage companies (and many larger mortgage companies have their own title departments onsite) – there are also thousands of smaller mortgage and title companies who are employed not only to do the title search but also to notarize the documents for a loan closing. Therefore, mortgage and title companies do employ independent notaries to fill this need. It is up to you to find these types of mortgage and title companies who are located in your area and market your services to them, or you may

wish to work for a nationwide mortgage or title company but you will be competing with professionals who
"know the ropes". My suggestion would be to stick with
marketing to local mortgage and title companies until
you know you have the ability to compete in the professional market with the "big" boys and girls.

The following is a list of easy-to-follow steps for
notary signing agents to begin marketing their notary
services to mortgage and title companies.

Step 1: Make Sure You Have Experience

Before you begin contacting mortgage and title
companies directly you need to perform an honest self-
evaluation of your experience. If you have just become
a notary public and have never completed a loan signing, you do not want to contact mortgage and title
companies at this point in time. You need to gain
enough experience so that you at least know the basics
before contacting them.

The reason for this is because you normally only
have one shot in the real estate market. It is very easy
to damage your reputation and it could take years for
you to climb back up. If you have no knowledge of loan
signings and you contact mortgage and title companies
at this point in time, your inexperience will be very
apparent to them. Not only will they not give you any
work, but you may never obtain work through them
even when you do become experienced. So play it safe
and have some experience under your belt before you
proceed.

Step 2: Put Together a Marketing Package

Next, you need to create an effective marketing
package that you will fax to mortgage and title companies. Your marketing package should consist of the
following items:

Your Resume

The resume you will use to fax to mortgage and title
companies should be a resume that reflects your real-
estate and notary experience. Do not include unrelated
job experience such as any factory employment, community service, etc. Instead, design your resume to
include experience you have obtained in an office environment, any clerical skills or other skills that are
relative to processing paperwork and/or meeting the
public in a professional setting.

Many people make the mistake of taking a general
resume and sending it out to a professional business
hoping to obtain contract work. One thing you need to
keep in mind is that YOU are a business owner now.
You own a notary signing agent business and you are
the boss. The mortgage and title companies you are
going to contact must be treated like your customer.
Your resume should be rewritten in an attempt to show
the mortgage and title company what your services can
do for them.

But don't get carried away and write your resume
like a sales letter either. Many people think selling a
service is the same thing as selling a used car. They

will use words like: *"We're the best."* and then wonder why the company never calls them. The truth is, a sentence like *"We're the best."* is insulting to any company. The company should be the one to determine whether you are the best or not. Anyone can make that claim (and most of them often do). So instead of saying *"We're the best."* try saying something more customer-oriented like *"We'll do our best to provide your company with high-quality professional services or your money is refunded. No questions asked!"* This statement shows the customer you really back up your statements and it will create more trust between you and the customer than simply saying *"We're the best."*

On Page 129 is an example of a typical resume a notary signing agent might use to market their services to mortgage and title companies.

Of course you should add as much relative information as possible to your resume, but the example on Page 129 provides you with a basic template to get you started. Notice that your company resume is not set-up like a personal resume you send out to employers when you are seeking a full-time job. Instead, the resume you send to mortgage and title companies to market your notary signing agent business should be short, to the point, and only include relative information the mortgage or title company would find necessary in order to make a decision to contract your services as a notary signing agent.

Develop a Cover Letter

Next, you need a cover letter that is personalized with the name and address of every mortgage and title

Jane Doe
Jane Doe's Notary Services
Certified Notary Signing Agent
123 Main Street
Bluff City, Tennessee 37618
Phone: 423.555.2121
http://www.janedoesnotaryservices.com

Summary of Experience:

♦ Owner of Jane Doe's Notary Services; a company dedicated to notarizing loan documents for mortgage closings. Some of the companies Jane Doe's Notary Services has processed loan documents for include DiTech, Beneficial Bank, CitiFinance and many others.

(Notice that Jane Doe did not list the name of signing companies she worked for. This is because when Jane accepts an assignment from a signing company, the actual mortgage documents were initiated by the mortgage company – i.e., DiTech, Beneficial, etc. Therefore, Jane is really processing loan documents for a mortgage company already. The signing company is only the "middle man." Mentioning the names of the mortgage company carry much more weight than a signing company will).

(continued)

Sample Resume Page 1 of 2

♦ Three (3) years experience as an Administrative assistant in a busy real estate office, coordinating documents for agents actively involved in commercial closings.

♦ Seasonal employment as a customer service representative working directly with consumers and following-up to resolve matters of dispute.

Certifications and Education:

♦ Certified Notary Signing Agent, Certificate awarded by the National Notary Administration, http://www.nationalnotary.org (2003)

♦ Real Estate training course, Jacksonville College (1998)

References available upon request

Sample Resume Page 2 of 2

company you will be faxing your marketing package to. On Page 132 is an example of a cover letter you can use as a template to write your own.

Notice that the letter is written as a soft-type sales letter. It is not written like a used car salesman who is using high pressure sales techniques. The letter is professional, it provides the company with an outline of the benefits of hiring you and it guarantees your service 100%. All of these points are essential in writing a good cover letter that will certainly help in getting the attention of mortgage and title companies.

Copy of Your Business License

Although you do not need to apply for an EIN (employer identification number) to own and operate a notary signing agent business, you may want to obtain a business license in your state. A business license is normally obtained through the Secretary of State's office and the cost is normally under $20.00 in most states.

To find the location of where to obtain a business license in your state, go online to http://www.sba.gov/hotlist/license.html

If you do not have a business license and do not wish to apply for one, you can still fax your marketing package without it. However, if you do have one – the business license will show you are established and help to present your company as someone the mortgage or title company may be able to form a long-term business relationship with. All companies look for the "cream of

Jane Doe's Notary Services
123 Main Street
Bluff City, Tennessee 37618
Phone: 423.555.2121
Fax: 423.555.1212
Email: owner@janedoesnotaryservices.com
http://www.janedoesnotaryservices.com

May 28, 2005

Mr. Johnny Appleseed
Manager, Loan Closing Department
Big Daddy Mortgage Company
PO Box 1111
Skipper, ND 67555-1111

Re: Notary and Loan Closing Services

Dear Mr. Appleseed:

As a Certified Notary Signing Agent, experienced in the
notarization and processing of a variety of first and second
mortgage loan documents, I am interested in providing
notary contract services to Big Daddy Mortgage Company
on an "as needed" basis.

I am sure you recognize the convenience of having
access to an independent notary signing agent who is
experienced in the loan document signing process.
Instead of contracting with a signing company to dispatch
a notary who may or may

(continued)

Sample Cover Letter Page 1 of 2

not complete the documents to your specifications, employing my services on an "as needed" basis would increase the efficiency and accuracy of processing your loan documents since I would become familiar with your procedures and operations. Additionally, I am available on very short notice, which is another convenience signing companies often cannot provide.

Enclosed is a copy of my resume and notary commission to verify my credentials. I would welcome the opportunity to meet with you at a convenient time. Or, please feel free to contact me for your next closing. My services are 100% guaranteed.

Thank you for your time and consideration.

Sincerely,

(sign your name in blue ink here)

Jane Doe
enclosures

Sample Cover Letter Page 2 of 2

the crop" when selecting an independent notary to close loans for them. Do whatever is necessary to show the company you are the "cream of the crop" so you can get their business. And after you get their business, continue to improve your services and never take their trust in you for granted.

Copy of Your Notary Commission and/or Certification

If you have passed the certification course through the National Notary Association, you may want to include a copy in your marketing package also. Your Notary Commission Certificate will also provide immediate verification that you are a notary public commissioned in the state you reside in.

Step 3: Locating Mortgage and Title Companies

Now that you have put together a professional marketing package you need to locate mortgage and title companies to fax your information to. The best place to start is in your local Yellow Pages phone directory. Look under "mortgage companies," "title companies," and even the "real estate" section to locate mortgage and title companies in your area.

Write down the company name, street address and telephone number of the mortgage and title companies you find in the telephone directory. Next, call each one and ask them the following question:

"Could you tell me the name of the person I need to speak to that is in charge of loan closings?"

Depending on the personality of the receptionist and the workload he or she is under at the time of your call, the receptionist may immediately give you the name of the department head as well as fax number without hesitation. These are the easy calls.

But I often found that some receptionists would want to know what type of materials I was faxing before they would provide me with any information. I would reply with direct answers such as: *"They are materials relating to notary public services."*

If the receptionist continued to question me, I normally would say something like: *"I am a notary public and I am interested in speaking to the person in charge of having documents notarized after the approval of a loan."* Normally this would get me the information I was seeking. If not, I would disconnect the call and call back later during lunch. Between 12:00 and 1:00 every day most office staff employees go to lunch. You can often call during this time and get an answering service who will immediately give you the information without question.

Another technique is to call a company after they have closed for the day. Sometimes the answering machine will give you an option to go to the company directory. If you have this option, take it. Listen to the list of names and select one to call tomorrow. When you call back this time and the disgruntled receptionist answers the phone, you can say something like *"Hello. This is Jane Doe. May I speak with Johnny Appleseed please?"* Once you get Johnny Appleseed (or whoever) on the phone, you can ask them to direct you to the person in charge of the closing of loans after they have been approved.

You may be wondering "why" you should go through all this time and trouble locating the name and fax number of a specific person at a mortgage or title company to fax your marketing package to. The answer is simple – you will get assignments faster. Think about it for a moment. If you send your marketing package to anybody at the mortgage company, do you think the employee receiving the fax will really care if the right person receives your information or not? When I worked in an office outside my home, if we received an unsolicited fax (a fax with no specific person's name on it) we tossed it to the side. Although this may not happen in all offices, the chance of you getting your information to the right person will be diminished unless you spend the time and trouble now sending your marketing package to the specific person in charge of loan closings at the mortgage or title company.

When you have ran out of listings in your local telephone directly for mortgage and title companies, the next step is to locate more on the internet. Most mid-size and larger mortgage and title companies have offices in many different states. You can send your marketing package to these companies if they process mortgage loans for borrowers within your state or county jurisdictional limits. As long as you call them first (or check their website) to make sure they handle loan closings in your area, you can market your notary services nationwide to the big companies.

To get started in your internet research:

1. Go online to Google at http://www.google.com

2. Type in the search words "mortgage company"

3. Start visiting the websites of mortgage companies and look for contact information. First try to find out if they process loan closings in your area. Next, look for the name of a specific person, their fax number and mailing address so you can use this information to send them your marketing package.

Have fun! It could take months to work through all the mortgage companies listed on the internet. But think of all the work you will have when you are finished. You may even need to team up with another notary signing agent in your area just to keep up with the additional workload. So during the time you are contacting mortgage and title companies, try to build a business relationship with several other notaries in your area to help you handle the overload. If you hang in there – you will see the results of your hard labor. Believe me! This is the same method I used when I worked directly for mortgage and title companies and I know you can do the exact same thing.

Step 4: Prepare a Professional Fax Cover Page

Believe it or not, the appearance of the cover page you use to fax information to companies is as important as the information in your marketing package. Always strive for professionalism in all your printed materials.

You want them to present the same image you present to borrowers when you arrive at their home in professional business attire.

On Page 139 is an example of a Fax Cover Page template you can use to create your own.

Step 5: Fax Your Marketing Package

The order in which your marketing package should be faxed is the following:

1. Fax Cover Page
2. Cover Letter personalized for the mortgage or title company
3. Your short 1 or 2-page resume
4. Notary Certification and/or Notary Commission

Also, you may want to fax your materials after 2:00 pm and avoid faxing on a Monday or Friday. There have been many surveys conducted that claim the majority of office workers are less attentive to their duties on Monday and Friday. They are also less attentive in the morning and peak during the afternoon hours after they have returned from lunch.

Of course you do not necessarily need to adhere to this line of reasoning, but you should still pay attention to the time of day you are faxing your marketing package to the mortgage or title company. If you try to fax your marketing materials and get a busy signal, this indicates the fax line is tied up at the moment. You may want to wait up to an hour before you try faxing

**Certified Notary
Signing Agent**

FAX

Victoria Ring, CNSA
50 STATE NOTARY
1601 W Fifth Ave #123, Columbus OH 43212
Voice: (614) 491-9831, Fax: (614) 491-9832
http://www.50statenotary.com

TO: **Johnny Appleseed
Big Daddy Mortgage Company**

FAX NUMBER: **800-555-1111**

FROM: Victoria Ring

DATE: August 27, 2004

NUMBER OF PAGES 5 (including this cover sheet)

NOTES:

Mr. Appleseed:

I have been informed that you are the manager of the
loan closing department at Big Daddy Mortgage Company.
I am interested in working as an independent notary for
loan closings in the Franklin, Licking and Union county
Ohio areas. My resume and other materials are attached
for your review.

Thank you for your time and consideration.

CONFIDENTIALITY NOTICE:

This message may contain confidential and privileged information.
If you have received this message by mistake, please notify me
immediately at **614-491-9831,** and do not review, disclose,
copy or distribute this message. Thank you.

Sample Fax Cover Page

again in the hope that your fax receives the attention it deserves. You certainly do not want your marketing package to get lost or misdirected, which is why you should do a follow-up call, which we will cover next.

Step 6: Follow-Up

What separates the good marketers from the mediocre ones is the ability to follow-up on their marketing. Many people will often go through all the right steps to market their business but never follow-up with a simple phone call or email. These same people wonder why they are not getting any assignments when all they had to do was take 10 minutes and follow-up by email or telephone.

Make sure you keep a list of all the mortgage and title companies you have faxed your marketing package to. Also be sure to write the date you faxed the package beside their name. Wait approximately three (3) working days after you have sent your fax and call the person on the telephone. Say something like: *"Hello, my name is Jane Doe. I am the notary that faxed you a letter and information on (date). I was just following up to make sure you received my fax."*

Notice that you are NOT trying to sell your services. You are simply giving a courtesy call to check and make sure your fax was received. If the person is interested in your services, he or she will probably engage into a conversation with you at this point. Be prepared to answer questions in a positive manner about the benefits of your notary signing agent service and always

remember to maintain a professional attitude, regardless of how the person on the other end of the telephone is behaving.

Step 7: Don't Give Up

Marketing is all about using a variety of methods to
sell your services to other companies. Don't contact
one mortgage company then sit back and wait for them
to call you with an assignment. Get in there and fax
your marketing package to every single mortgage and
title company in all the counties that you cover as a
notary. Eventually a company will hire you as an independent notary .. so don't stop until you have accomplished your goal.

After you start working directly for a mortgage or
title company, you will be able to add more to your list
of customers. The first sale is always the hardest to
make. After you have done that, building your business
will become much easier.

Special Resource You Can Contact Immediately

I must give credit to Deborah Densmore of Alabama
Notary Services for providing the following valuable
information. Please visit Deborah's notary website at
http://alabamanotaryservices.com

1. Go online to http://www.irepvm.com/

2. At the top right is a login area. Below the login
area is a "Learn More" button.

3.   Click on the arrow immediately to the right of the "Learn More" button and select "Interested in Becoming an IREP Vendor" from the drop down menu. It is the last selection on the menu.

4.   You are taken to a Vendor Application form under the URL http://www.irepvm.com/ default.aspx?page=14

5.   Fill out the Vendor Application. For "Business Type" select "Closing Company" as your option. (In some states a notary signing agent has the title of Closing Agent instead of Signing Agent).

After this process you should receive a set of documents entitled "Independent Loan Closer Closing Instructions." Make sure you read them thoroughly and understand everything perfectly. Never be hesitant to call the company if you have any questions. It is better to ask questions now than to make mistakes later that could cost the borrowers hundreds of dollars. Besides, a company is very impressed when you call to ask questions. It shows them you are conscientious about your work and want to do a thorough and professional job.

Note: Deborah informed me that she had to negotiate her price per signing when she initially signed up with IREP. Because all companies will attempt to save money any way they can, it is important for you not to settle for $50 or $60 per loan closing. Instead, you need to negotiate a figure that is comparable (but slightly lower) than what the signing companies charge.

The way to find out the normal amount to charge for your area is to look at the HUD Settlement Statement and find the amount paid in closing fees. In some states, this figure may be as high as $400 or $500. In other states the average may only be $150 or $200. Therefore, make sure you know the average rate for your area and negotiate your fee using this average figure as a guideline.

Unfortunately, the truth of the matter is that mortgage and title companies do not actually pay the closing fee. They may pay the notary directly but ultimately the borrower is the one who pays the fee, so there is no money coming out of their pockets. Why companies continue to discredit the value of the notary public by paying them $40 or $50 is beyond me, especially since they are not actually paying the notary – the borrower is.

Are you Legally Inclined?

A final suggestion for enhancing your notary signing agent business is to add a bankruptcy forms processing service. You can still work from home but you will be transferring information provided by a debtor onto the federal bankruptcy forms. You work directly for bankruptcy attorneys across the United States because you have no jurisdiction limits like you do working as a notary in your state. To find out more about this rapidly growing field (due to the massive rise in bankruptcy filings) order a copy of my book, "How to Start a Bankruptcy Forms Processing Service" at http://www.bankruptcybook.net.

Who is a wise man and endued with knowledge among you? let him shew out of a good conversation his works with meekness of wisdom.

James 3:13

SECTION 5

Questions and Answers

And this I pray, that your love may abound yet more and more in knowledge and in all judgment;

Philippians 1:9

Questions and Answers

The questions below are from actual notaries who emailed me during the past year. Below each question I provide my personal answer. I am sure this information will help answer many of the questions you may have after reading this book.

QUESTION: Hello, Victoria. You were very kind in helping me decide whether to spend the money to take a training course to be a notary signing agent or not. I followed your example - studied on my own and passed.

I wanted to ask your opinion about something else. I got a frantic call from a title company in Maryland last week, asking if I was available for a refinance signing that evening in Minneapolis. I was given 3 hours notice on this. I agreed to do it and drove to the client's house about 20 miles from me. The refinancing was a variable interest rate - the rate changed after 2 years. The client stated that he did not agree with that rate and it was not what he was quoted. I advised him to contact his lender - he left a message but the lender had gone home for the day.

I contacted the title company and told them what happened and said I would be available to go out again if needed. They said they'd let me know because they "weren't sure" when the next closing would be. Since then, I've heard nothing and I'm wondering if you think I should be paid for this. Perhaps not the full fee but I did use about 1½ hours of my time to do this and it was not my fault that the documents were not correct. This is my first signing so I would be interested in what you think. Thanks so much for your time.

ANSWER: First of all – congratulations on passing the test and earning your Certified Signing Agent certificate. There are some people that need additional training before taking the test, but it basically is common sense and I am glad you took the "bull by the horns" and did it. Good for you!!

Moving along to the next issue – I totally agree with you! You should be paid even though the signing did not take place. Normally when you sign up with the company, there is a paragraph stating the amount they pay a notary if the client refuses to sign. First, you need to check the paperwork the company supplied you with when you signed up with them to see if this issue is addressed.

If there is no information, contact the company right away. Ask to speak with a supervisor – not the person who answers the phone. Ask them what their company policy is concerning paying notaries who travel to a borrower(s) home but the borrower(s) refuses to sign. Allow the company to give you their policy before you proceed. If the company states that you are still paid for showing up at the signing – explain that you were not paid and at that time you can request payment.

In the future, it would be to your benefit to find out the company's policy concerning a situation like this before you elect to sign up with them. Personally, I tried all the signing companies and found most of them to be uncaring toward me as a notary. However, after "kissing a lot of toads," I did find a couple of really good companies that kept me busy, paid me on time and paid me for signings where the borrower(s) refused to sign.

QUESTION: I am a notary and I signed up with your Nationwide Notary Directory about a month ago. I stay pretty busy with the signing agent business. Most of my work comes directly from title companies who pay on time and I usually get between $125.00 - 200.00 per signing. A lot of these signing companies want to insult me by offering me $50.00 with e-documents included.

I am training two other notaries to do this so they can take some of the pressure off me. I love working at home and on the internet. People have often told me how resourceful I am with finding out information by accessing the various state and county records. My question Victoria is this: How can I turn my ability to locate any information into a homebased business?

I have friends that call me when they are checking out the background of potential mates, tenants and real estate. You name it – I can find it. As we all know, most county records are public info, but most folks think they have to go downtown and search the records themselves. I look forward to hearing from you.

ANSWER: Good for you girl! I am very happy that you "get it" and you don't allow other companies to walk all over you and pay you low fees for a signing.

To answer your question though – your gift, desire and ability to locate anything about anyone can be utilized in so many different ways, we could spend several months brainstorming and still not cover the options available to you.

However, to get you started thinking on their right path – you could use your ability to go into virtually any area of law as a paralegal. Or, you could attend law school and become a law clerk since attorneys and judges pay law clerks excellent salaries to research and find information relating to their case. Many attorneys may even pay you as a subcontract to their law firm regardless if you are a paralegal, law clerk, or have no legal experience but you will need to sell the benefits of your service to them to get the job.

There is also a bid demand for investigative skills in the medical profession as well as the collection field. In addition, there are several thousand websites that provide services to the general public for locating relatives, deadbeat dads and more. You may want to locate some of them and offer to work as a subcontract under them so they will refer business to you.

QUESTION: I have just taken the notary exam in Xenia, Ohio. I was notified I passed the exam and am waiting for notification as to what is next. The goal to all this is to be a signing agent. But really Victoria, at this point, I need an honest opinion.

To take the course at the National Notary Association and become a member is another $200.00 dollars rounding it out. Do you really feel that if a person is a go-getter they can make this work? I don't have previous experience in title work, real estate or mortgage work.

I don't mind the class or the investment and I love learning this material and it does take time. I wouldn't mind continuing my education to assist in my career development for the rest of my life. My hesitation is whether I will be hired. I've read through many web sites now and they allude to hiring people with experience. I don't want to go into this and really spend the time and money to hear, "unless you have experience we cannot use you".

I've had this happen before and just couldn't bare it or the financial depletion again. I want to be proactive toward my own goal of a successful rewarding career and financial bounty to take care of myself this life. Please help me by mentoring me through this with your true feelings.

ANSWER: As far as investing additional monies into notary education, that would be a choice you need to make. I do not know you and therefore cannot answer this question. Some notaries really need the education because they don't even know how to place documents inside a Fed-X envelope, seal it and deposit it in the proper Fed-X box (this is true). While other people can pick up the signing agent business from "on the job" experience.

You also can go to our notary directory at http://www.50statenotary.com/directory/index.html and email other notaries in your area so you can network with them. Since notary regulations are different in each state, it would be best to contact a notary in your area who is familiar with them.

As far as needing experience before you can go on a notary signing – I have never had this problem. The first signing I did, the company was aware it was my first one and they trained me over the telephone. With my legal background, I only had a couple of questions about the documents as to how the company wanted them processed. I hope this helps and I wish you the best of success.

QUESTION: I am a first time notary and NSA. I surfed the web and found your website. I enjoyed reading it. When you notarized for hospitals and convalescent homes, who paid you and how much did you charge?

ANSWER: You are not permitted by law to charge any higher fee than the courthouse charges in your area to notarize documents. This information should have appeared in the notary laws of your state that should have been issued when you obtained your notary commission. If you lost this information, call the courthouse and find out how much they charge to notarize documents and write this information down.

You will find that in most states, the amount you can charge to notarize documents will be very small (normally $1 or $2). But if you travel to the notarization, you may charge an additional fee for your travel-related expenses.

When I notarized documents at hospitals and convalescent homes, I charged $1 for the notarization and
$10 for the travel expenses. If I had to travel outside
my county, I charged $25 or more for travel expenses.
The fee is paid by the person (or family) who had you
notarize the document. You only need to have contact
with the hospital or convalescent home one time to let
them know your services are available. Most hospitals
and convalescent homes will have a notary public onsite
and available during normal business hours. But since I
was willing to notarize after hours and on weekends, the staff would pass my name along to any resident
who needed a notarization after business hours. The resident or resident's family would contact me directly.

QUESTION: I am writing about a new web site that
I have created at http://www.notarybeware.com. This
site was created to be a one-stop web site for notaries
to check for deadbeat signing companies as well as
those that pay well. I got tired of logging into all the
notary web sites out there (and can't afford to join them
all at $20+ a year for membership) just to see who
pays and who doesn't. After talking to several notaries,
they agreed it would be great to have one site. The
cost of membership is $5.00 per year. This cost will
maintain the site online and upgrade it as needed. Let
me know what you think.

ANSWER: I visited your website and must con-
gratulate you on the design. However, I do want to
share an experience with you that may be beneficial to
your situation. Back in 1992 when I published The
GrapeVine News, I decided to list companies who had

ripped people off through mail order. People would send me their complaints and I would print them in each monthly issue.

But it turned out that many of the people submitting the information about companies ripping them off were not legitimate complaints. Instead, the majority of them only wanted revenge or to "get back" at someone they didn't like.

That is when I decided to allow every company I received a complaint on to tell their "side of the story" before I published anything negative about them. When I received a complaint, I would mail a copy to the company for their rebuttal. I would provide them ten days in which to respond or the information would be published about them. In your case, I would also provide the company with your website address to show you mean business.

Using this method may even help your website to make a "real" difference in resolving legitimate complaints. By you directly contacting the company who has received the negative complaint and letting them know the negative information will be published unless they resolve the matter or contact you with an explanation – they may pay the notary monies due them in order to avoid the risk of "bad press."

QUESTION: I just recently started notarizing loan documents and I noticed the penmanship of the borrowers is illegible. Will I get put in jail because I notarize documents with bad penmanship?

ANSWER: Your job as a notary is to identify the borrower(s) and make sure the documents are properly signed. You should also have the borrower(s) sign your Notary Journal and in many states it is also best to take a thumbprint. Your job is not to judge how poorly a person writes their name. That is irrelevant!!

QUESTION: If the borrower is not home what should I do? Wait 30 minutes? Go home? Wait one hour then go home? Call the escrow? Please advise.

ANSWER: You should never encounter a situation when the borrower is not home. That's because you should have contacted the borrower as soon as you accepted the loan signing, introduced yourself and obtained directions to his or her home. You also should have called the borrower on the day of the signing to confirm the time you were to meet with them to sign their paperwork. Finally, you should have provided the borrower with your telephone number so they could call you if an emergency came up and they needed to reschedule.

It appears you did not do any of these steps or you would not have encountered this situation. About the only solution when you find yourself in a situation like this is to contact the lender and find out what they want you to do. This is one reason a cell phone is necessary for all notaries to have on them at all times.

QUESTION: I am a newly commissioned notary in Minnesota. In applying online to various signing companies (which I found through your website - thank you),

many of them want you to list your social security
number or driver's license number on the email sent
back to them. I am not sure if these emails are en-
crypted and secure so I am hesitant to do this online.
What do you think?

ANSWER: I am sure this issue is debatable with
other notaries, but personally I have never had a problem giving out my social security number or driver's
license number to title, mortgage and signing companies I sign up with online. But then again, I am used to
providing this information all the time on legal documents because it was required information when I
worked as a paralegal.

However, if you are uncomfortable with giving out
any personal information on the internet – then don't do
it. Instead, you can always print out the form, fill it out
and fax back to the company. The companies need your
social security number before they can pay you because
they will issue a 1099 at the end of the year to file with
your taxes. But whether you provide that information in
a fax, online or by telephone is a decision you will need
to make for yourself depending on your level of comfort.

QUESTION: How do you feel about notaries going
out to the homes of borrower(s) alone? Have you heard
of anyone getting victimized?

ANSWER: I had an interesting conversation with a
notary in the state of Florida a couple of months ago.
She told me about an incident where a notary was
called out to do a loan closing and she was actually

---

murdered. This notary had arrived at an address only to discover it was a field containing only one dilapidated old barn. Instead of turning the car around and driving back to a secure area, she drove up to the property and actually got out of her car. Suddenly, two people ran out of the barn, raped her and shot her in the head. It took almost two months to find her.

My reason for repeating this story is NOT to scare you. Instead, you should be aware and take some simple precautions to protect yourself from the possibility of this happening to you. Here are some ideas:

▶ Designate one friend, relative or neighbor to be your "business tracker." Whenever you have a closing scheduled, always leave the address of the borrower(s) home with this designated person and call them when the signing is completed so they will know everything went well and you returned safely.

▶ Take your spouse or partner with you to the closing. They do not have to meet the borrower(s). They can simply sit in the car and wait for you since most signings normally take only 30-45 minutes.

▶ Network with other notaries who serve the same areas you do and take them with you on signing appointments. You can both go to lunch or dinner afterwards and share tips with each other. To find a notary in your area, you can go to my online directory at http://www.50statenotary.com/directory, click on your state, select a county you serve and immediately contact other notaries in your area!

▶ Find a newly commissioned notary and offer to train them if they accompany you on a signing. This way – you both benefit.

▶ Always call the borrower as soon as you receive their contact information. Have a general business conversation with them and "feel them out." If you are uncomfortable in any way, offer to meet the borrower(s) at a quiet restaurant close to their home or invite them to your office if you have one. Do not go to any signing appointment alone that you feel uneasy about.

Personally, I have never encountered a situation where I felt uncomfortable going to a borrower(s) home and notarizing mortgage documents. Most of the borrowers I have met were kind, warm and receptive people who treated me with respect. I would think the majority of people are anxious to close their loan and move on with life – so a notary should be a welcomed visitor. But keep in mind, there are satanic idiots that exist on this planet. I am sure they are not above using fraudulent identity to get approved for a loan and then harming the notary. Some of these nuts have been known to shoot the pizza delivery guy – so anyone is a target for insane people like this.

QUESTION: My thinking concerning the problems with non paying outfits, is if you get another signing from them, tell them to have the borrower(s) pay you the notary fee at the signing. What do you think?

ANSWER: You better read the contract you signed when you initially signed up with the company who sent you out on the signing assignment. The method of receiving payment from the borrower(s) versus the company you signed up to work for – may not be permitted. If you freelance for a company, you have made a contract with them in performing a service for a set fee. Violating that contract could cause you to end up in court.

Think about it this way. If you signed up with a temporary service (i.e., Kelly Girl, etc.) and went to work for a company, you know you are to be paid by Kelly. If you approach the person you are doing the work for (Kelly's customer) and ask for your pay – it would violate your contract with Kelly.

Although a signing company is not a temporary service – the contract you enter into is similar. If all notaries were permitted to obtain their payment from the borrower(s), it might result in the notary being paid twice (once by the borrower and once by the mortgage company). It would also be impossible for companies to track "who" got paid by the company and "who" got paid by the borrower(s).

Therefore, either check your contract or call the company before proceeding with a request from the borrower(s) to pay your notary fee. I believe it could get you in trouble.

QUESTION: I just recently completed a signing for a signing company in Florida. The documents were emailed to me by the title company. The signing went just fine but I made a mistake and thought it said on the HUD Statement that cash was to be paid to the borrower(s). However the title company called and told me I had to go back out there and collect the funds.

This occurred on a Saturday. Needless to say I could not contact anyone at either company. The borrower(s) wanted to know exactly what the "cash from borrower(s)" was for. I could not answer this question because I didn't know and I think this should have been explained prior to my arrival the first time.

Now the signing service says I will not be paid because the funds were not collected. I can deal with that but what about the expense of my travel and also the documents being emailed to me? What do you think I should do about both my situations? This could not happen at a worse time.

ANSWER: You ALWAYS need to check Lines 303. 1601 or 1604 of the HUD Statement for any signing you do prior to the appointment. If money needs to be collected from the borrower(s) and you do not collect it upon the notarization – the loan will not close and the whole process (as well as new documents) may have to be redone again. This is probably why they will not pay you. Was there a reason you didn't just drive back out to the borrower(s) home and collect the check and overnight it at your expense back to the company?

All you can do at this point is chalk it up to experience. You made a mistake that everyone has made at one time or another. At least you will remember the next time to check the HUD (Settlement Statement) before going on another assignment. Some closings require money to be collected from the borrower(s). The payment normally must be in the form of a money order or cashier's/certified check or money order. The borrower(s) should have already been informed of this – but if not – you need to check the HUD statement, call the borrower(s) prior to the appointment to give them time to go to the bank or other establishment in order to get a cashiers/certified check or money order. (Most companies do not accept a personal check for a loan closing due to the fact the funds can bounce. A money order or cashier's/certified check is a guarantee the check is good).

When a loan closes, the borrower normally receive money back. However, in some cases, they have to pay. Learning from the "school of hard knocks" is not a pleasant experience but it makes all of us better at our jobs.

QUESTION: I recently obtained my notary certificate and signed an Independent Contractors agreement with a local notary company in Sacramento, CA. They sent me out Friday on my first assignment COLD TURKEY??? I did not realize there were about 50 pages for the client to either sign or initial. Somehow I got through it and when the package was reviewed the only thing I did wrong was not stamping clearly, and missing one state and county on a split notarial wording on one page. I was a bit stressed over the matter.

In my opinion the best training would be for someone to create a DUMMY loan package and as an assignment have you and another person sign and initial wherever necessary and for the notary to notarize and fill in the wording. Then the whole package could be double checked and any errors pointed out to the notary. The stamp could be anything, not your legal stamp.

Anyway your notary web site is THE BEST I have found on the internet. Great work and God Bless.

ANSWER: Your idea would work seamlessly "IF" all mortgage documents were the same for every loan. However, there are thousands of different types of loans. In fact, every single mortgage loan is unique because all borrower(s) have different situations. For instance, if the property is NOT located in a flood zone area, the flood-related document would not be required as part of the loan package. Or suppose the property was located in two different counties? This would create additional paperwork that would NOT be applicable to other mortgage loans where the property is located in only one county.

So you see – there cannot be any one training course developed that would include instructions for every single document in a loan package. (In addition, documents also vary from state to state). The only solution is to provide training for documents that are "normally" part of all loan packages, such as the HUD Statement, Note, Mortgage, etc., which I have included in this book.

After reviewing the major documents you will understand that the mistakes you made were VERY

serious. You describe them as *"the only thing I did
wrong was not stamping clearly, and missing one State
and County on a split notarial wording on one page."*
These simple mistakes could have resulted in the loss of
hundreds of dollars, depending on which document you
are specifically referring to.

I realize that this was your first signing and you
were thrown into it "cold turkey." Given this situation I
would say you did a pretty good job. All you need to do
now is to educate yourself so you can do a better job
next time.

QUESTION: The state of Virginia is one of several
states that do not offer a "certified" test for Notary
Signing Agents. Do you have any recommendations on
how we experienced (but uncertified) Notary Signing
Agents can promote our experience and professionalism
other than boldly announcing "I've signed over 510
loans in the last eleven months."

ANSWER: I have received several emails from
notaries concerning this same topic so I called the
National Notary Association to find out the reason why
some states are not eligible to obtain the "Certified"
notary signing status.

For future reference, the Notary Signing Agent
Certification is currently not available in the following
states: Georgia, Louisiana, Massachusetts, Maryland,
North Carolina, North Dakota, South Carolina, South
Dakota, Virginia and West Virginia. This is due to the
laws of those particular states that have tough requirements in place for notaries who do closings. These state

laws include requirements such as obtaining a state-issued bond, or the notary must be an attorney, title or insurance agent, etc.

The National Notary Association stated that if the notary meets the requirements for their state to conduct closings, they would consider issuing a certification test on a case-by-case basis to notaries commissioned in the states listed above. But since most notaries do not meet these tough requirements, the NNA cannot super-cede state law and offer the certification to everyone in those states.

QUESTION: I can only find companies willing to pay $40 for a signing. What am I doing wrong?

ANSWER: I consider myself to be very blessed because I have the opportunity to talk every day to notaries across the United States about their signing experiences. It is interesting ... one call will be from a notary complaining because she did not receive her check for $40 from a company she did a signing for three months ago – and the next call will be from a notary sharing his excitement with me about the $250 signing he did for a title company.

Now ... there is a BIG difference between $40 and $250. And because of this huge difference, this indi-cates there are two different worlds that notary signing agents work in. Either these two different worlds exist because new notaries do not have the experience to negotiate their fee higher than $40, or the company is set up to "take advantage" of notaries and make a huge profit for their signing company.

One of our subscribers to <u>The Notary News</u> faxed me a copy of the Proposed NSA Fee Schedule published in Volume II, Issue 2, Winter 2003 edition of NSA Today. The fee schedule indicates the following:

Certified Signing Agent Minimum Fees
- ▶ $65 – First set of loan documents
- ▶ $35 – Second set of loan documents
- ▶ $85 – Emailed loan documents
- ▶ $35 – Cancellation (2 hours or less)

Noncertified Signing Agent Minimum Fees
- ▶ $50 – First set of loan documents
- ▶ $25 – Second set of loan documents
- ▶ $75 – Emailed loan documents
- ▶ $25 – Cancellation (2 hours or less)

Unfortunately, companies are not required by law to adhere to these fees. So if they can find a notary who will do the job for $40 they will continue paying these extremely low wages. One solution to regulating these companies would be for the NNA to require the companies to become certified like the notaries are. Once certified, the company would operate according to the rules established as "fair for all" by the NNA and receive the benefit of referrals from the NSA of experienced and certified signing agents. This way, the notary would have the choice of either working for a "certified" company or not. If the notary chooses to work for a company that is not certified through the NNA, they would be taking their own chances.

Whether or not my idea will ever become reality or not is still unknown. But as notaries, we CAN do something right now to help stop these low-pay signings. The solution is very simple! Either negotiate a higher fee or DON'T ACCEPT them. Remember, you are a freelance notary public running your own business. You have business expenses just like any other small business. You serve the public and you are a respected member of the community.

You do not deserve to spend several hours fighting to get all the documents for a signing, then rush out the door, dodge traffic, get the documents signed, fill out the journal, notarize the documents, come home and fax certain documents back to the company for confirmation, rush to find a Fed-X or UPS drop-off box, come home and prepare your invoice and then "hope" you receive a measly $40 within the next 30 days. It's ridiculous. And you should laugh at any company that would offer you $40 for all this work.

But a small percentage of notaries have a mindset that other people are going to steal assignments from them. In other words, they believe if they turn down an assignment because it pays only $40 – that someone else will get the job. They also believe that if they turn down an assignment that the company will never call them again. All of these reasons are nothing more than fantasy. The world of business does not operate like that. People that think like this need to direct their attention toward improving their skills so they can work "up the ladder" to the jobs that pay $250 or more per signing. Instead, they spend all their energy worrying about $40. What a waste of energy, time and creativity!

Also, some notaries feel that any amount of money for performing a public service is sufficient. This line of thinking is true if someone comes up to your door to notarize a simple car title that takes about 15 seconds of your time. But the NSA business is different. Mortgage documents can contain up to 150 pages (depending on the particular loan). Also, there are several documents to notarize (instead of just one). Besides, the fee for the notary is included in the HUD Settlement Statement and paid for by the borrower(s).

Anyway – this information is meant to encourage everyone reading this to demand more than $40 for any signing assignment. Do not be afraid to ask the company how much you will be paid for the assignment (this is common procedure) and if they quote you a price of $40, just say, "My fee is a minimum of $____. " The company normally will negotiate a price between both figures and you can accept or decline the job. If you are afraid to take this step of negotiation, then you will have to stay imprisoned in this low paying world until you decide to make a change. I wish you the best.

QUESTION: I am interested in meeting other notary signing agents in my local area and networking with them as you suggested in your newsletter. How can I get started and what are the start-up costs?

ANSWER: The cost to you is free or very minimal and you can charge a membership fee to cover the costs associated with the group once it is has been established. The purpose of a local notary group would be to discuss problems, find solutions and form valuable friendships for referring business back and forth to each other.

If you have a spare room, den or basement you could hold meetings at your house. When a friend of mine in North Carolina started her group, she contacted notaries in the area and everyone met at Denny's Restaurant for dinner and held their first few meetings. After the group began growing, she rented space at the local library for only $10 per meeting. The membership fees each member paid were $25 per year, but the first two meetings were free. This caused more people to attend a free meeting before joining and she generated more memberships since people found the meeting valuable.

You can begin by contacting notaries in your area through our Nationwide Notary Directory at http://www.50statenotary.com/directory/index.html. Send an email to notaries in your state expressing your interest to start a local notary group. Ask them to provide you with a date and time that would be convenient for them. Once you get back two or more responses, schedule a time and meeting place and hold your first meeting. Be sure to send me an email and let me know how it goes.

QUESTION: If more notaries join the NNA will that hurt me as a notary signing agent?

ANSWER: I was shocked to receive a few emails from signing agents who wanted my opinion about whether they should renew their membership with the National Notary Association (NNA). It appears that some notaries feel membership dues are being spent to advertise for new notaries to compete in an already overloaded refinance market."

If this is how you feel – or if you know anyone else who feels this way, I strongly urge you to pass along the important information below. This article has also been published on a variety of internet websites.

A Lesson in Understanding Competition

If you were a notary who lived in a town with a population of 100 and there were 200 notaries in nearby areas who serviced your small town, your fear of competition would be well founded. However, if you lived in a city with a population of four million – and there were 200 notaries serving that area, NOT one of those 200 notaries would need to worry about competition. That is because each one would have enough work to keep them busy 24 hours a day. In fact, those 200 notaries couldn't keep up with the demand of a city containing four million people, so the only way to meet the needs of the city, the 200 notaries would need to increase their number by recruiting more notaries to help them.

Do you think the 200 notaries would be upset and angry because more notaries offered to help serve the four million people? Of course not! They are already so overwhelmed with the demand, they would welcome the extra help and would be more than willing to train the new notaries or answer any questions they have. That way – all 200+ notaries effectively work together to

serve the needs of the four million population. They
don't "knit pick" and look at each other as competition.
Instead, they see themselves as the member of a large
group with a goal in mind of serving the general public
(which is what a notary public is supposed to do).

Now that you understand this example – expand the
four million number to include the entire population of
the state you live in. Do you know the population of
your entire state? If not, I am sure it is more than four
million. This should make it easy for you to use the
example I provided to see for yourself that NO notary
signing agent is in competition with anyone. There is
enough work for you and thousands of other notaries
within your state without thinking about competition
from others. Therefore, instead of "knit-picking" over
something that doesn't exist – you should be helping
new notaries learn how to do their job properly and
networking with others so all notaries within your state
can serve the public in a professional and legal manner.

Many notaries get into the signing agent business
thinking this is some type of "business opportunity."
Your first goal as a notary public is to SERVE the public
– not gripe about whether or not Jane Notary did the
signing for Joe Borrower's mortgage loan. It's more
important that Joe Borrower(s) loan was professionally
and legally processed by a notary who cares about the
quality of the work he or she performs.

QUESTION: What recourse do notaries have when
they complete a signing and never get paid?

ANSWER: There are two websites dedicated to exposing fradulant companies who do not properly pay notary signing agents:

▶ My Notary Business
http://www.mynotarybusiness.com/

▶ Notary Beware
http://www.notarybeware.com

Becky Bergman (owner of My Notary Business) is a professional journalist from SFSU with more than six years writing experience as well as being a notary public. Becky is one of the pioneers in developing a web business dedicated to exposing warnings about companies who do not properly pay notaries. Becky said: *"I know how to research and report fairly and accurately. While I post all claims - no matter how they are resolved, I give companies two business days to respond before posting the claim online and if they refuse to respond or fail to live up to their agreement, I post all relevant information on my Warnings Page. If the company resolves the issue, I post the follow-up so that readers may see how the case was resolved and how long it took."*

MyNotaryBusiness.com also offers a wide range of features including notary-related articles, mentoring (not just for signing agents but for all notaries interested in volunteering/requesting a mentor) and work-at-home related material. In the coming weeks, Becky said she would be introducing articles and resources on title abstracting, home inspections, mortgage loan origination and much more.

QUESTION: I feel negligent in my work in not helping the borrower understand the individual documents better, since they are not having it explained by the lenders (which baffles me). Many borrowers are really in the dark as to what they are signing. I was taught that we were not to explain documents, that we were only there to witness the signing but if there was a pamphlet they could refer to during the three day right of recission it would make some of them more aware of what they are doing.

ANSWER: I feel the same way you do – but in most states you are prevented from explaining documents to the borrowers. I understand that your heart is in the right place and you have a concern for other people – but the government and man-made law doesn't.

Normally what I do is hand the borrowers a document. I will say something like *"This is the Truth in Lending Statement. You need to sign your name on this line."* (point at the line). Most of the time, the borrowers never ask any questions. They are normally only concerned with getting the paperwork signed so their loan can close and they already know the details of their loan prior to approval.

If the borrower stops to look at a piece of paper, I allow them time to do so. If they have a specific question that is not related to UPL (unauthorized practice of law), I normally will answer it for them. If I am unsure about violating UPL or not, I will say *"Every loan is unique and different. Let's call the company and find out.*" Then I will call the signing company and hand the phone to the borrower to ask their question directly and remove myself from the middle.

QUESTION: The things I do not enjoy about being a Notary Signing Agent are: Waiting for documents to download and faxing signed docs at the end of a signing. I also do not like faxed HUDS that are sent after the original docs are received. Sometimes waiting for these documents have caused me to have to juggle my time between signings. This is very stressful as I like being in control of my time. I have lost jobs due to the lateness of downloading documents. I think companies should have the documents before they hire a notary.

ANSWER: I totally AGREE with you. The docs should be ready in time for you to make the appointment but this rarely happens because of all the different people involved in the mortgage loan process. Getting everyone to come together with their documents at an appointed time is often impossible for signing companies. For some notaries, the things you mentioned on your list are enjoyable or tolerated without stress. In fact, many notaries look at your list as challenging and exciting.

But this doesn't mean that you should not listen to your feelings. You, I and a host of other notaries have felt exactly the same way you do at one point in their career, but it all boils down to recognizing and identifying the things that you enjoy doing. Life is meant to enjoy – not to create stress. The first step to taking charge of your future is recognizing "who" you are and

what you enjoy doing. Then you can take steps to form
your business around your own personality.

In your particular case, you may want to begin
seeking other areas of the real estate and legal field
that would better fit your working preferences. Notarizing documents to close mortgage loans is only the "tip
of the iceberg." There are literally millions of other
ways you can utilize your skills in this industry – you
just would be doing a different job in another area.

The real estate industry is vast and wide open with
possibilities for maintaining steady work. But you will
need to spend time researching the different fields until
you find one that fits you. I cannot tell you what "that"
is because I do not know you. I can only offer ideas so
you can research them for yourself. But the real fun is
discovering what exactly you enjoy doing and what
direction you want your business to take.

I urge you to seek other avenues that better fit your
lifestyle and working preference. If you are not enjoying
what you are doing, your business will suffer and possi-
bly be destroyed. You must LOVE your business in
order for it to grow and prosper so you can become
financially independent.

QUESTION: I have been consistently asked to have
a borrower backdate a document from mortgage companies, title companies and signing agencies. My
response to these requests has been equally consistent:
*"The borrower can sign any date on the documents they
so choose. However, any documents that I notarize need
to reflect the date I'm doing the actual notarization."*

I am then told that they do it all the time and they would pay a higher fee for me to do it. When I refuse again, I say, *"It is illegal for me to do that and I'm unwilling to jeopardize my commission by backdating the documents."* At this point they apologize and say they will get another notary to do it. It doesn't cost me future assignments, the company respects my morals and principals, and I respect my commission, my work and most importantly, myself.

However, herein lies the major problem: there are other notaries willing to do this. Do they realize if the borrower disputes the signing for any reason, and then 'exposes' the fraudulent notarization, the notary will lose their commission and can be sued? Is this really worth the extra $50? I don't think so. Whether or not it is common practice for some companies, it's against the law. By accepting a commission to become a notary public, the notary has taken an oath to uphold the law. If the notary cannot abide by those terms they should relinquish their commission.

ANSWER: This is very excellent advice. I will pass this along to other notaries in the Second Edition of How to Start, Operate and Market a Freelance Notary Signing Agent Business. I am sure that many people will benefit from your information. Thank you.

QUESTION: I was given a split signing and received the documents today. I called the title company to ask about the right-to-cancel date and was told not to change them – and that since the husband signed on the 12th it would be okay to back date the documents.

I know this is incorrect and I refused to back date any of the docs. The title company called the signing company and I was again asked to back date by the signing company. They also said I was told to do so at the acceptance of the order.

I explained to both that it is against the law to back date documents and I would not do it. I was then told they would have someone pick up the documents and someone else would do the signing. Isn't there a way to report signing companies and title companies to law authorities and stop this illegal back dating? Also, the notary who picks up these docs will also be back dating docs and breaking the law.

But the story gets better. I received a call from the other notary who was going to do the job I refused to do. When I asked him if he back dated docs, he finally realized what they were really asking him to do. He called the NNA about the issue and got the same answer I did. He then called the signing company back and refused to complete the signing.

Then I received a call from another notary who said she does back dates docs all the time. In fact, she has an affidavit they sign releasing her of any responsibility, saying as long as the title company, loan company and the borrowers agree – it's okay. I told her she was wrong and gave her the NNA article plus the article published in The Notary News and suggested she read them. She threw them back in my face. This is what we are up against. Notaries who know they are breaking the law and getting away with it. This puts us all in a bad light.

ANSWER: Good for you! You deserve a big pat on the back for sticking to the law and conducting your business as a professional should. The reason the notary who back dates documents threw the articles back in your face is simply because she is greedy. She does not want to know the truth because it will make her face the fact she is operating a fraudulent and unlawful business. Remember, people who are greedy and operate in a fraudulent manner do NOT want to hear the truth. Instead, they will get mad just like this lady did. These are the types of people you want to stay away from. They will do nothing to help you in business. They are only known for destruction.

QUESTION: Victoria, did you know that title companies compare notes on your performance as a notary? Yeah, neither did I, but they call your "signees" and other notary and title companies and check you out. They want to see if you behave and dress professionally, if you are polite and friendly, if you are on time, and if you follow instructions well. I just wanted to give a "heads up" to others so they can upgrade their performance.

ANSWER: You got it! And that's how things work in almost any industry. As you know, the real estate market is a competitive market. It really is a "who knows who" environment and unless a notary provides high-level, professional service – information concerning their level of performance will always be passed from vendor to vendor so they can "weed out" the bad and save time.

This is one reason "why" some notaries are not making any money as a signing agent. In the majority of cases I spent time researching, I found that the notary did something wrong during the document signing process. Either the notary did not present a professional image with the company as well as the borrowers, or the notary did not properly process the documents.

Often, any problems related to not properly processing the documents can be solved by training the notary. I also found that many of the notaries who made these mistakes had absolutely no knowledge of basic notary public rules and regulations. However, I am unable to provide you with a "quick fix" for upgrading your professional image. That is something you will need to observe and learn from other professionals.

QUESTION: I was contacted by a signing company and was asked to accept email docs for a signing that was to occur on July 28th. Also, I was told the documents would be ready by 12:00 noon.

I was called on the 27th and told the closing was for that day not on the 28th. Also, they could not give me any idea when the docs would be ready. Right after that, another person from the title company called with incorrect borrower information (different name and town) and said that I was scheduled to do the closing on July 27th at 5:00.

After the time problem was straightened out, I was asked to do a split signing on the closing. (Husband only available the next day but wife would sign on closing date). I was also asked to back date the husband's signing. They actually told me the wife was available the next day with the husband but if I felt more comfortable with at least one of them signing on the closing date they would be glad to pay me for both dates.

I was speaking with a person named Veronica who spoke very professionally but was a bit brisk and short. When I started asking questions and suggesting we do both on July 28th as originally scheduled, she asked if I would like for her to look for another notary. I told her to see what she could straighten out with the dates and call me back to let me know when the docs would be ready.

She called me back and told me she did not know when the docs would be ready and rather than string me along all day, she would just find another notary. That was the first time they had called me and I had never heard of them before. I was wondering if you had a situation like this occur.

ANSWER: It sounds like this is an internal communication problem. This scenario could occur with any company you work for.

Please try to understand that just because a signing company issues you a set of mortgage documents, this does not mean the signing company prepares the documents. Instead, there are often many different companies with their "hands in the pie" in any one mortgage.

Often it is impossible to get all the companies to send
their portion of the documents that make up the loan
package at the proper time, which causes the signing
company to be placed in the middle of a situation they
have no control over.

While "back-dating" documents is illegal – as a
notary signing agent, you need to remain flexible and
attempt to work with the companies by understanding
their dilemma. This is called building good customer
relations. It is rare that any loan signing will always go
smoothly. However, if the company consistently lies to
you and shows a total lack of concern – simply do not
accept any more assignments from them and don't do
business with them again.

QUESTION: My husband and I were driving down
the road and my cell phone rings. The lady identifies
herself as the person I had done a signing for a few
weeks before. It turns out, she and her husband were
in the real estate business but the signing was separate
from that issue. Anyway – she had called up because
they had some connections with local real estate offices
and wanted to put me on their list for doing such
signings. The potential for such exposure is huge.

ANSWER: You are correct! The potential for exposure as well as jobs for notary signing agents is very
huge.

Unfortunately, many people want to start off making
$200 or more per signing working for title and mortgage
companies without any experience. They do not want

to take the time to build up a high-quality reputation because "money" is placed higher on their list of priority than "quality". Evidently the real estate people were impressed with your level of professionalism. They could recognize your attention-to-detail, honesty and ability to do the best job possible just by your mannerism.

This is one reason why it is so important for any notary to be professional, honest and willing to do a good job for any borrower or company they come into contact with. Word gets around fast and no one will respond to negativity.

It's amazing how many arguments I have overheard where the basis of the argument is someone telling the other person what to do. There are only two ways to get someone to change their behavior and do what you want them to:

1. If the person agrees with you.
2. Under force and/or bribery.

So if you believe a negative attitude is going to help you get what you want – think again. Unless the person agrees with you or unless you scare them to death – you are not going to get accomplished what you want to accomplish.

QUESTION: I decided to try the signing agent business approximately a month ago I am now commissioned and have purchased various supplies and training materials (your wonderful book included).

Being a single mom and a full time worker, I have not had much time to review the materials; however, I was just laid off from my job this past Monday and thanks (in great part) to your positive advice, outlook and thorough explanations of the business I am considering giving the signing agent business a 100% try.

Since I need an income ASAP, I appreciate your feedback concerning the time frame needed in order to start making money and the income possibility considering the market as it is today. Should I pursue 100%? By the way, although I have not read much of your book as of yet, I can already tell by the way you present the knowledge that you have gained and the fact that your spiritual belief has great influence in your work, that you are a great mentor for anyone trying to prosper in this as well as any other field that you may have some knowledge of. THANKS so much! Please advise.

ANSWER: I am very sorry to hear about your job loss. I too have suffered through a few job losses in my lifetime (even filed bankruptcy in 1986); so I know how devastating it can be. It may help you to know that millions of people are in the same position you are in right now. The world is moving into a direction that is squeezing out the "blue collar" worker. Many jobs appear to be moving out of the U.S. and unfortunately the innocent people must suffer.

As far as me advising you whether to pursue the notary signing agent field or not – I am unable to do that. Only you can make that decision. All I can do is provide you with the tools I know that worked for me. You will need to decide for yourself if you will pick up the tools and use them or try something else.

The main thing to keep in mind is to find something you enjoy doing and that you are good at. You should never enter any field of business with the sole intention of making money. It would be better to work at McDonalds for minimum wage than to start a business you do not personally enjoy working at.

I am sure after you do a few signings you will be better able to decide if this is the field you want to work in – and I hope you make the decision to stay with us.

QUESTION: Can you tell me what prices to charge for doing a title search?

ANSWER: No, I cannot tell you what price to charge for anything you do in your business. That would be the same thing as Wal-Mart telling JC Penny what prices they should charge in their store. You need to keep in mind that YOU are a business owner. It is up to you to price your products and adjust them as necessary. But keep in mind that it is easier to LOWER a price than to RAISE it.

Determining prices to charge for your title search business can be obtained in a couple of different ways:

1. Do a search on the internet for title companies in your area. Visit their website and find out how much they charge for their service.

2. Do a "test" title search on your own property or the property of a friend of relative. After you have completed the title search at the courthouse, you will know approximately how long it will take to do the job and the expenses involved. After you have come up with a total for your time and expenses, add on about 25% to the price for a "cushion." This should help you to determine a better price to charge for your service and if the price is too high, you can always run a "30-day special offer," lower the price and probably get more business. Just make sure you never RAISE your price.

QUESTION: Why does it matter if I dress professionally or in normal attire when I do a closing at a borrower's home? We are not in a business setting.

ANSWER: The way a notary dresses can actually cause havoc during a signing. For instance, I trained a new notary a few months ago. I asked the notary to meet me at the signing appointment versus me picking her up at her home. When she arrived at the appointment she was dressed in a very low-cut blouse which is very unprofessional. However, I did not say anything because I knew she had not worked in an office before and probably had no concept of proper office attire. But when we walked up to the borrower's home and the husband answered the door, his eyes immediately went to the revealed cleavage. The notary did not seem to notice it, but the wife sure did. In fact that low-cut blouse set a negative mood for the entire signing. Additionally, the husband and wife didn't even talk with the new notary. Instead, they addressed all their questions to me since I was dressed in professional business attire and had the mannerism of a professional.

But the low-cut blouse was not the only problem with this new notary. Because the husband and wife were directing their attention to me and I was doing most of the talking, the new notary never once tried to join in the conversation. She sat back, her eyes wondered around the room and she appeared as if she didn't care about anything we were saying. Again, this added more negative energy to the room and everyone was anxious to move through the process as quickly as possible and get both of us out of there.

After leaving the appointment I met with the new notary privately and asked her for her feedback concerning the signing. (Notice, I did not immediately bring up her mistakes. I allowed her the opportunity to provide me with feedback first so I could better assess the situation and understand where she was coming from). She said: *"I was scared to death. I could never do a signing myself."* The solution now became simple. I told her to find something else to do for awhile. A good idea would be to get an entry-level job in an office and build her confidence in working with people. Through this experience she would also learn how to dress, pick up some tips on office etiquette and adapt a body language that portrays a sense of calmness and creates a relaxed atmosphere for the people around her.

Dressing professionally for a signing appointment is not the only key to success as a notary signing agent. I have gone on a few late-night appointments in casual business attire compared to wearing my 3-piece suit – but it was because the appointment was an emergency and I did not have time to prepare. But the major key

is presenting yourself as a confident professional who
enjoys what they are doing and showing concern and
compassion for the borrowers. I have watched some
notaries treat borrowers like they were nothing to them
but a quick way to make a buck. Turn the situation
around. Pretend the borrower is someone like your
mother, sister or best friend. You would certainly treat
these people with more concern, patience and love than
a stranger. Now, treat the borrowers the same way and
you are on the road to better success.

QUESTION: I contacted a few notaries in my area
who were listed in the 50 State Notary Directory and
was told there were not many signings in my area.
These notaries also said they only received two or three
calls per month for a signing assignment and were not
making much money at all. Could this be true?

ANSWER: It would be impossible for me to answer
this question. I did not speak directly to these notaries
and I do not know what marketing techniques they have
implemented, so determining whether they were telling
the truth would be an impossible task for me.

However, if a notary told me he or she was only
receiving two or three calls per month for signing assignments; I would immediately question his or her
marketing techniques. I would first ask them how many
companies they were registered with? If they didn't
provide a number of more than 150, I would wonder
why they stopped marketing. If a notary signing agent
is only receiving two or three calls per month, they
should be seeking out new companies to sign up with

on the internet every day. There are literally thousands
of companies to sign up with. Signing up with all of
them should keep you busy for the next eight to ten
months so I do not understand why some notaries
complain about not getting enough work and then never
spend every spare moment marketing on the internet.
It is a totally bazaar thought to me especially since
marketing is free on the internet and marketing is what
will bring you money!

On a final note, any city or town that has real estate
for sale (which is just about everywhere) needs a notary
to notarize the mortgage documents. If you are not
getting enough work as a notary signing agent it is
probably because you are lacking something in your
marketing techniques. Try to find the problem and
correct it immediately.

In the meantime, watch who you accept advice
from. If you try to network with notaries in your area
and they present negative information to you – find
notaries who will inject positive information for you to
build your business on. Try to seek out the professionals, the winners – the people making good money in
this business. These are the people you want to learn
from. Not people who have no knowledge or willingness
to implement sound marketing techniques in growing
their business.

QUESTION: I don't have the money right now to
purchase the National Notary Association certification
course. What can I do to earn money between now and
then?

ANSWER: I have no idea who started this untrue rumor that a notary must be certified by the NNA to notarize loan documents. YOU DO NOT NEED TO BE CERTIFIED to begin notarizing – all you need is to be a notary public. In fact, the day you file your commission with the state, you can start signing up with companies and begin working.

If you cannot afford to purchase the certification course offered by the NNA at this point, work for a few companies to earn the money to become certified.

Becoming certified by the NNA has many terrific benefits and you normally can obtain more money when you accept a signing appointment. However, it is not a requirement and if you hear this rumor again – put a stop to it. It's only a rumor dreamed up by someone without any experience or knowledge of the industry.

QUESTION: How much competition does a notary signing agent have in this industry?

ANSWER: According to an article I read this past week in a business magazine, it is estimated that approximately 80% of the notaries have no idea the notary signing agent field exists. That is because most notaries believe they are limited to $1 or $2 for a notarization and they think getting paid $125 or more for a signing is nothing but a scam.

Even with these facts, some notary signing agents still call and ask me how much competition they have just like you did. I tell them they have "NONE" but they are still worried the market is oversaturated with notary signing agents and cannot seem to see the big picture. In the big picture – all of us are on the cutting edge of a booming industry. Everyone has a chance to make some excellent money right now – so stop waiting and get involved before you miss the bandwagon and are left behind with the other 80% who will join in the future.

Although California has the highest number of notary signing agents registered on the various online directories – California is a huge state. You cannot compare a state like California to a state like New Jersey or vice versa. Just because California has more notaries – the averages are the same if you compare land mass to land mass.

I urge everyone to stop worrying about competition and fretting over these little details that do not matter to a hill of beans. Sometimes a person can research so much that they become frightened into thinking they do not have the experience to do a closing. Then, these people will sit back and wait – then complain they are not making any money. I say, *"Start working! Jump in and do it!"* Besides, if you have any questions during a signing, you can call the company while you are at the borrower's house. Or, if you are scared to death to jump in – at least make an effort to contact other notaries in your area and go on a signing with them.

I had a notary email me this week about this very subject. She said she loved training new notaries. One day she received a call from a notary that said she would like to go on a signing assignment with her. The notary agreed to help but then the new notary said: "*I won't even charge you anything.*" This statement was totally uncalled for. The experienced notary who emailed me said she flatly refused to help this person. Instead of feeling like she was doing a favor for the new notary, the new notary presented it like she was doing her a favor.

Therefore, if you do reach out for help – be professional and courteous. It is YOU who are seeking free training. The least you could offer the notary is a free meal for spending time training you. It should never enter your mind to believe you are doing the other notary a favor. This is not rationale and courteous thinking.

SUBSCRIBE TO
THE NOTARY NEWS!

If you enjoyed the information in the preceding Question and Answer section, you will love every issue of <u>The Notary News</u> because many of these questions and answers appeared in previously published issues. To subscribe, go online to
http://www.50statenotary.com/
type your email address in the subscribe box
and you'll receive the next issue.
You can unsubscribe at any time.

SECTION 6

Web Site References

*No mention shall be made of coral, or of pearls: for
the price of wisdom is above rubies.*

Job 28:18

References on the Web

The following pages contain a list of all the web references in this book. I urge you to spend the time going through them and utilizing the information to benefit your notary signing agent business.

National Notary Association
http://www.nationalnotary.org/join/index.cfm?
referID=A23039

Signing Agent
http://www.signingagent.com/
SigningAgent.Com is owned by the National Notary Association. Get listed in this nationwide directory and gain access to title and mortgage companies seeking freelance notaries.

Tips for Learning Non-Verbal Behavior
http://www.selfgrowth.com/articles/Albright2.html
Excellent information if you are just getting started in business.

Nationwide Notary Directory
http://www.50statenotary.com/directory/
order_getlisted.html
Get listed in this directory and other mortgage, title and signing companies will call you for freelance assignments when they are needed in your area.

NSA Weekly
http://www.nsaweekly.com/
A free online publication for Notary Signing Agents

Field Inspector
http://www.fieldinspector.com/
Search the database for field inspector job opportunities.

Home Inspection Success Book
http://www.homeinspectionsuccessbook.com/

Mortgage Ramp
http://www.mortgageramp.com/
Click on "jobs" and sign up to do home inspections.

Notary Public Training Seminars
http://www.notarytrainer.com/
Find a training seminar to improve your skills as well as network with other notaries.

The Notary Law Institute
http://notarylaw.com/
Excellent resource for notaries to improve their skills with continuing education.

Locate a Notary Mentor in Your Area
http://www.mynotarybusiness.com/mentor.html

Tools for Notary Signing Agents
http://www.mynotarybiz.com

PACER Service Center
http://www.pacer.psc.uscourts.gov/

Find Your Local Court
http://www.findlaw.com/11stategov/

Health Insurance for the Self-Employed
http://www.anthum.com

Low-Cost Prescription Medication
http://www.rxnorth.com

Title Abstractor Training
http://www.learnanytime.net/title.ab/
http://www.nationalabstract.com

Bummer Hosting.Com
http://www.bummerhosting.com
Web hosting service I personally recommend.

Checking Availability for Domain Name
http://www.networksolutions.com

Developing Your Own Web Site

Free Web Page Tutorial for Absolute Beginners
http://www.freewebmastertips.com/

Full Reference Online Web Design Tutorials
http://www.w3schools.com/
http://www.pagetutor.com/

HTML Goodies (only designed for people who understand hand coding)
http://www.htmlgoodies.com/

Online Resources for Web Designers
http://www.sitetutor.com/

Web Reference Articles
http://webreference.com/authoring/design/
tutorials.html

Submitting Your Web Site to Search Engines
http://www.addme.com/
http://www.bizweb.com/InfoForm/
http://www.canlinks.net/addalink/
http://www.google.com/addurl.html
http://dmoz.org/add.html
http://www.submitexpress.com/
http://www.worldsubmit.com/

Internet Power Marketing
http://www.internetmarketingconference.com/
http://www.dotfactor.com/
http://www.onlinewebtraining.com/
http://www.searchengineworkshops.com/
http://insite.lycos.com/tutorial.asp

Notary Accounting Software
My Mobile Notary
http://www.thefelicita.com/

Download Your Own W-9 Tax Form
http://www.irs.gov/pub/irs-pdf/fw9.pdf

Adobe Acrobat Reader
http://www.adobe.com/products/acrobat/readstep.html
Must be installed on your computer in order for you to
accept edocs from mortgage, title and signing
companies.

Information on Starting a Small Business
http://www.businesstown.com/
http://www.isquare.com/
http://www.powerhomebiz.com/
http://www.businessownersideacafe.com/
http://www.businessnation.com/
http://www.allfreelance.com/start.html
http://www.workathome-com.com/
http://www.entrepreneur.com/

Overnight Envelope Supplies
http://www.ups.com
http://www.fedex.com

Office Supplies
Calendar System
http://calendar.yahoo.com

<u>Note</u>: Microsoft Works, which is already installed on
most computers has an excellent calendar program also.
Click on START > Programs > Microsoft Works >
Microsoft Works Calendar. There is also a database and
other utilities but you will not be able to access the
information from any computer like you could with
Yahoo (see above).

Business Cards
http://www.businesscards.com
Use the design wizard to make your own business card
online before ordering.
<u>Also check out</u>:
http://www.vistaprint.com/
http://www.business-cards.com/

http://www.weprintcolor.com/
http://www.bizcardsxpress.com/

Notary Directories
http://www.123notary.com
http://www.50statenotary.com/directory/
http://www.usanotaries.com/
http://www.gomobilenotary.com/
http://www.accuratesignups.com/

Business License Information
http://www.sba.gov/hotlist/license.html

Keep Updated on Fradulant Companies
http://www.mynotarybusiness.com
http://www.notarybeware.com

50 State Notary's Website

CD-Rom Notary Training Videos
https://www.50statenotary.com/videotraining/

FREE: 50 State Notary Desktop Guard Dog
http://www.50statenotary.com/freegift/

Locate a Notary: View the Nationwide Notary Directory
http://www.50statenotary.com/directory/

Jobs for Notary Signing Agents (updated weekly)
http://www.50statenotary.com/directory/
company_listing.html

View previous issues of The Notary News
http://www.50statenotary.com/ezine/

Free Introductory Signing Agent Training Course
http://www.50statenotary.com/training/index.html

My Notary Story – Tips from Experienced NSAs
http://www.50statenotary.com/mystory/index.html

Free Download of the King James Bible
http://www.servantofjesuschrist.com/

Visit Victoria Ring's other websites
http://www.victoriaringconsulting.com/
http://www.graphicopublishing.com/
http://www.bankruptcybook.net

Ministries Supported by 50 State Notary

Bible Baptist Church
http://www.kjv1611.org/

AV Publications, Corp
http://www.avpublications.com/

Creation Science Institute
Dr. Kent Holvind
http://www.drdino.com

And now come I to thee; and these things I speak in the world, that they might have my joy fulfilled in themselves.

St. John 17:13

Building Your Skills in Internet Research

As previously mentioned, there are thousands and thousands of resources listed on the internet seeking independent notaries for a wide variety of jobs in the real estate industry. Since you are the only person who knows exactly what you enjoy doing and what skills you have – you will need to continue researching the internet on your own. One of the main reasons people do not take this step is because they don't know how to properly search specific topics on the internet — so let me help get you started.

Let's suppose you wanted to find opportunities for notaries to earn more money. I have known some people to go to a search engine and type in the search words: "notary" and then get upset because they can't find anything. The problem is not the search engine – it is the words you used to do a search. You must be more specific. Try typing in something like "jobs for notaries" or "notary jobs" or "notary sign up form" or even "how to make more money as a notary" so you can get better search results and find the information you are seeking faster.

Every search engine has either an "Advanced Search" a "Preferences" area or a "Help" section to assist you in targeting the topic you are researching. For instance, go to Google (http://www.google.com) and on the RIGHT side of the search box there are links for "Advanced Search," "Preferences," and "Language Tools." Click on these links and you will see what is available to you. Yahoo' search engine also has help information available at http://help.yahoo.com/help/us/ysearch/, as does MSN, Alta Vista and many more.

Another search engine some people like to use is Ask Jeaves at http://www.ask.com/. You can type in your search in the form of a question. For instance, I typed in *"How do I make more money as a notary signing agent?"* and received some excellent results to start my research.

When you are able to target your words and get the results you want from the search engines, begin clicking on the links and visiting the websites. If you don't find anything of interest at one website, look for resource links or links to other websites. (Most websites have a links section to continue your research). If you find something in this list of links of interest, check it out and continue the process. As you dig deeper into the internet you will encounter many different worlds you never knew existed and this information will open up doors of opportunities you never realized were there.

Summary

I hope you have enjoyed the information contained in this book and will put it to good use to build your own notary signing agent business. I look forward in hearing about your progress in the near future.

Victoria Ring
Certified Notary and Paralegal

About the Author

Victoria Ring is a freelance writer and self-publisher living in Columbus, Ohio. She has written 22 books, hundreds of articles and five training courses for paralegals and notaries since she opened her first publishing business in October 1988.

Victoria specializes in the writing of "how-to" information in a variety of subject areas including: internet marketing, small business management, new business start-ups and web design. Utilizing Victoria's 24 years of legal-related experience she also writes and publishes materials for paralegals, notaries and attorneys. Victoria also developed a set of Client Intake Forms for bankruptcy attorneys that are still being utilized by law firms nationwide.

Aside from writing, Victoria enjoys studying God's Word and developing a better relationship with Jesus Christ. She is involved in the study of creation science (the belief that God created the world and we did not "evolve") and is a graduate of the Creation Science Evangelism college course instructed by Dr. Kent Holvind in Pensacola, Florida located online at http://www.drdino.com/.

Victoria is a Certified Notary Signing Agent through the National Notary Association, a member of the Paralegal Association of Central Ohio, associate member of the Columbus Bar Association and member of the Publishers Marketing Association. Victoria's formal education in writing was obtained from Thompson Education Direct and she holds two Associates Degrees in Paralegal Studies and Business Management.

"Take heed, brethren, lest there be in any of you an evil heart of unbelief, in departing from the living God. But exhort one another daily, while it is called To day; lest any of you be hardened through the deceitfulness of sin."

Hebrews, Chapter 3, Verses 12-13

Other Materials by Victoria Ring

Books:

The Best of The Notary News - Volume 1 (2004)
ISBN: 0-9761591-3-9
http://www.50statenotary.com/ezine/book/

How to Start a Bankruptcy Forms Processing
Service (2004)
ISBN: 0-9761591-1-2
http://www.bankruptcybook.net

My Homemade Business (2004)
ISBN: 0-9761591-2-0
http://www.myhomemadebusiness.com

From Author to Publisher to Profit (2005)
ISBN: 0-9761591-4-7
http://www.graphicopublishing.com/book/

Older Business Books:

Business Advice for Beginners (1998)
ISBN: 1-5834504-4-0

More Business Advice for Beginners (1998)
ISBN: 1-5834504-5-9

Making Your Small Business Grow (1997)
ISBN: 1-5834560-3-3

Other Materials by Victoria Ring
Continued

Free Articles by Victoria Ring
http://www.victoriaringconsulting.com/articles/

Companies Developed by Victoria Ring
http://www.victoriaringconsulting.com/companies/

Publications Developed by Victoria Ring
http://www.victoriaringconsulting.com/publishing/

Training Materials:

Notary Business Talks with Victoria on CD
http://www.50statenotary.com/videotraining/

Introductory Signing Agent Training Course
http://www.50statenotary.com/training/

How to Prepare a Bankruptcy Petition on CD
http://www.lawyerassistant.com/cds/

How to Design Your Own Website on CD
http://www.lawyerassistant.com/cds/
webdesign.html

How to Make MS Word Software Work the Way
You Want it To on CD
http://www.lawyerassistant.com/cds/
ms_word.html

Christian-Related Materials

Original 1611 King James Bible
Converted to PDF, HTML and TXT formats
http://www.servantofjesuschrist.com/kjv1611/

Christian and Inspirational Articles
http://www.servantofjesuschrist.com/articles/

"Now we beseech you, brethren, by the coming of our Lord Jesus Christ, and by our gathering together unto him, That ye be not soon shaken in mind, or be troubled, neither by spirit, nor by word, nor by letter as from us, as that the day of Christ is at hand."

2 Thessalonians, Chapter 2, Verses 1-2

Victoria Ring's Statement of Faith

Scripture

I believe that the King James 1611 version of the Holy Bible is the preserved Word of God and I use no other translation! For more information, go to http://www.servantofjesuschrist.com/articles/ biblecomparisons.html.

Trinity

I believe in the tri-unity of God: that the eternal God manifests Himself in three entities: God the Father, God the Son, and God the Holy Spirit, and that these three are one God, the Alpha and Omega, the King of Kings, the Lord of Lords, the beginning and the end and creator of all living things. I believe in the incarnation and virgin birth of Jesus, in His sinless life, and in the sufficiency and substitution of His death on the cross for the sins of the whole world; His bodily resurrection from the dead and His ascension into heaven thus restoring all people to fellowship with God and eternal life in Heaven if they acknowledge Jesus Christ as the Son of God – not just a prophet or good "human" being flawed with sin.

Creation

I believe in the creation of the universe and all living things by a direct act of God, apart from any

---

evolutionary theory or other similar process. See Genesis, Chapter 1, Verses 1-31.

Fall of Man

I believe that the fall of man (separation from God) occurred in the Garden of Eden when Adam and Eve sinned against God. I do not believe that this sin was caused simply by Eve eating an apple (an apple is not mentioned in the Word of God). Instead, the sin Adam and Eve committed was much more devastating than that. Genesis, Chapter 3, Verses 2-6 tells us the "fruit of the tree" God commanded them not to eat of was a very special tree. When they ate of it, their eyes would be opened, and they would know the difference between good and evil. There is no "apple" I know of that could produce that effect, so I believe that mankind's "watered-down" version of Adam and Eve's sin to be completely false and blasphemous.

The Atmosphere and Age of Earth

I believe the atmosphere of the earth was much different before the flood that occurred in Noah's day. This is proven by how long the people lived during that period of time. (See a list for yourself in Genesis, Chapter 5) indicating the Earth had a higher oxygen content allowing people to live longer. After the flood, people began living shorter and shorter life spans. (See

Genesis, Chapter 11). Because of this fact, it is therefore impossible to trust carbon dating and any other man-made methods used to measure the age of the Earth. Instead, I believe what God tells us in the book of Genesis – the Earth is 6,000 years old and the flood occurred approximately 4,400 years ago – not millions and billions measured by fallible equipment developed by man and not taking into consideration the atmosphere before the flood that occurred in Noah's day.

During the flood is when God opened up the "fountains of the deep." The devastation during this time knocked the Earth off its axis which is why our Earth has a "wobble" to this day. And even though the scientists admit the Earth has a wobble – ask them to explain it without using the words "millions of years ago." By using these terms, scientists do not have to acknowledge a creator and they have a larger gap of time to try and prove God does not exist.

Existence and Location of Hell

I believe a real Hell exists and it is located in the center of the Earth. After Jesus died on the cross He decended into Hell to offer salvation to those who had previously passed. Jesus Christ tells us the location of Hell in Matthew, Chapter 12, Verse 40: *"For as Jonas was three days and three nights in the whale's belly; so shall the Son of man be three days and three nights in the heart of the earth."*

Also, throughout the Bible, any reference to Hell is referred to as "casting down", therefore Hell is certainly not "up." Man has tried to reach the center of the Earth and they have found the Earth gets hotter and hotter closer to the center. No one will ever be able to get there unless they die in their sins. Read Luke, Chapter 16, Verses 23-24 to understand more about what the atmosphere of Hell is like.

How to Escape Hell

The only way to escape Hell is to admit you are a sinner and trust in the Lord Jesus Christ to save you. Believing that the shedding of His precious blood on the cross, that Jesus served as a "lamb without blemish" and took upon Himself all the sins of the human beings previously born, living during His physical time here on earth and all persons born after His death so that we could have the gift of eternal life.

Nobody in existence can save you from Hell except Jesus Christ. Only by His grace are you saved – and the only way to obtain His grace is through faith. Too many people ask God to prove to them He is "real" before they accept Him. God is the ultimate power and deserves much more respect than that. He already sent his Son to die for you. What more do you want?

1. Admit you are a sinner.
Romans, Chapter 3, Verse 10:
"As it is written, There is none righteous, no, not one:"

2. Believe in your heart that Jesus Christ died for you, shed His precious blood, was buried and rose from the dead.
Romans, Chapter 10, Verses 9-10:
"That if thou shalt confess with thy mouth the Lord Jesus, and shalt believe in thine heart that God hath raised him from the dead, thou shalt be saved. For with the heart man believeth unto righteousness; and with the mouth confession is made unto salvation."

3. Ask Jesus Christ to come into your heart, soul and mind -- and know that after your spirit leaves your body you will be in Heaven to live in peace for all eternity with your creator, Jesus Christ.
John, Chapter 3, Verse 16:
"For God so loved the world, that he gave his only begotten Son, that whosoever believeth in him should not perish, but have everlasting life."

My statement of faith is provided as a means of witnessing to others. As a Christian, I believe the only thing that really matters in this life is the work we do for God. I hope you make the decision to accept Jesus Christ as your Lord and Savior.

*"Wealth gotten by vanity shall be diminished:
but he that gathereth by labour shall increase."*

Proverbs, Chapter 13, Verse 11

Jump-Start Your Business!

*With personalized consulting and training
services provided by the author, Victoria Ring*

If you are serious about jump-starting your business there is no better training you can receive than training from someone who has lived through the experience first-hand. Victoria Ring has built a successful notary signing agent business as well as a bankruptcy forms processing service from the "ground-up" and knows how to provide you with the tools you need to build a successful business.

Regardless of whether you are a beginner or experienced business owner, Victoria Ring is available for personalized training to help you. Consultation services can be scheduled for telephone training in increments of 15 minutes up to several hours. Or, perhaps you would rather come to Columbus, Ohio and receive onsite training at Victoria's office. Prices are available to fit any budget. For current prices and to schedule a consultation visit http://www.50statenotary.com/training/consulting.html

(this page intentionally left blank)

ORDER FORM

To purchase additional copies of this book for your friends, family, business associates or if you teach a notary training class, you will receive a substantial discount. See the pricing chart below:

Copies	Price Per Book
5-10	$15.99
11-49	$13.99
50-99	$12.99
100-199	$11.99
200-299	$10.99
300 or more	$9.99

ALL MAJOR CREDIT CARDS ACCEPTED
VISA, MasterCard, Discover, American Express
NOTE: Personal checks NOT accepted

TO ORDER

To prevent destruction of this book in removing this page, please provide the following information on a piece of paper and fax to 50 State Notary at:

614.801-1962

- Your Full Name
- Street Address for UPS Delivery
- City, State, Zip
- Telephone Number
- Credit Card Account Number
- Expiration Date of Credit Card
- Name on Credit Card
- Quantity you wish to order
- Title of book (we sell several)

or mail your information to:
50 STATE NOTARY
1601 West Fifth Ave, #123, Columbus OH 43212

Graphico Publishing
http://www.graphicopublishing.com